EXPO 2010

中国2010年上海世博会官方图册
EXPO 2010 SHANGHAI CHINA
OFFICIAL ALBUM

中国2010年上海世博会

EXPO 2010
SHANGHAI CHINA

EXPO 2010 SHANGHAI CHINA OFFICIAL ALBUM

Bureau of Shanghai World Expo Coordination

 China Publishing Group Corporation

A bird's eye view of the site
of Expo 2010 Shanghai China

World Exposition Shanghai China 2010

Type

Registered International Exhibition to
International Exhibitions Bureau

Theme

Better City, Better Life

Duration
May 1— October 31, 2010

Site Area
5.28km^2

EXPO 2010
SHANGHAI CHINA

Emblem

The emblem for Expo 2010 Shanghai China resembles the Chinese character "世" (meaning "the world") and has the image of three people holding hands, looking like a happy family. It symbolizes the big family of mankind in harmony and happiness, conveys the world expositions' notion of "understanding, communication, reunion and cooperation", and showcases the great efforts of Expo 2010 Shanghai China to focus on the humanistic core.

Mascot

The mascot for Expo 2010 Shanghai China, HAIBAO (literally "sea treasure"), is created from the Chinese character "人" (meaning "people"), which reflects the feature of Chinese culture and echoes the Expo's emblem design.

The blue color: implying inclusiveness and imagination, symbolizing China which is full of hope and potential of development.

Hair: resembling the rolling waves, lively and distinct, and explaining the mascot's home and origin.

Face: simplistic cartoonish expression, friendly and confident.

Eyes: big, round eyes, shining with expectation.

Body: round body, evoking beautiful feelings for harmonious life, cute and lovely.

Fist: the thumb is raised to praise and welcome friends from the whole world.

Big feet: standing firmly on the ground and giving strong support to the outspread arms, which implies that China has the capability and determination to hold a wonderful world exposition.

The structure of the Chinese character "人" implies mutual support and signifies that beautiful life needs our joint efforts.

Only by supporting each other and living in harmony between man and nature, people and society and people among themselves, can urban life be better.

The World Exposition Shanghai China 2010 is yet another mega event hosted by China following the Beijing Olympics. It attracts the greatest number of participants in the history of the World Exposition. By March 25, 2010, 242 countries and international organizations have confirmed their participation.

The Expo is themed on "Better City, Better Life", the first time for a World Exposition to focus on the issue of city. Centering around the theme, participants from all over the world will stage exhibitions, events and forums to discuss the development of cities, offer their visions for the future, and promote understanding, communication and cooperation between nations and between cultures.

Expo 2010 is to be held in a downtown area between Nanpu Bridge and Lupu Bridge along Huangpu River. It has a total area of 5.28 square kilometers, and tickets are required for admission to the enclosed area of 3.28 square kilometers. Out of the five zones in the enclosed area, Zones A, B and C are in Pudong, and D and E in Puxi.

Exhibitions, events and forums are three core components of the Expo. Theme pavilions, national pavilions, pavilions of international organizations and corporate pavilions are built by the Expo Organizer or participants who will stage exhibitions in these buildings based on their own cultural background and exploration of the theme.

During the Expo, about 20 000 performances will be given. These amazing events, sponsored by the Organizer or participants, also provide interesting interpretations of the theme.

Forums, which deal with the Expo theme most directly, are always a central part of Expo legacy and an important platform to look into the future. A Summit Forum together with a series of theme forums and public forums were and will be staged before or after the opening ceremony of Expo 2010.

Besides these core components, Expo 2010 also introduces, for the first time in the history of the World Exposition, two great innovations, i.e., UBPA and Expo Shanghai Online.

Expo 2010 is expected to produce a positive effect in the development of the world's cities and contribute greatly to the sustainable development of human societies.

Let's wish Expo 2010 Shanghai China a great success.

Preface

EXPO 2010 SHANGHAI CHINA
Confirmed participating countries and international organizations

Up to March 25, 2010, 242 countries and international organizations have confirmed their participation in Expo 2010

Countries

China, Afghanistan, Albania, Algeria, Angola, Antigua and Barbuda, Argentina, Armenia, Australia, Austria, Azerbaijan, Bahamas, Bahrain, Bangladesh, Barbados, Belarus, Belgium, Belize, Benin, Bhutan, Bolivia, Bosnia and Herzegovina, Botswana, Brazil, Brunei Darussalam, Bulgaria, Burkina Faso, Burundi, Cambodia, Cameroon, Canada, Cape Verde, Central African Republic, Chad, Chile, Columbia, Comoros, Congo (Republic of the), Cook Islands, Costa Rica, Côte d'Ivoire, Croatia, Cuba, Cyprus, Czech Republic, Democratic People's Republic of Korea, Democratic Republic of the Congo, Denmark, Djibouti, Dominica, Dominican Republic, Ecuador, Egypt, El Salvador, Equatorial Guinea, Eritrea, Estonia, Ethiopia, Fiji, Finland, France, Gabon, Gambia, Georgia, Germany, Ghana, Greece, Grenada, Guatemala, Guinea, Guinea-Bissau, Guyana, Haiti, Honduras, Hungary, Iceland, India, Indonesia, Iran, Iraq, Ireland, Israel, Italy, Jamaica, Japan, Jordan, Kazakhstan, Kenya, Kiribati, Kuwait, Kyrgyzstan, Lao People's Democratic Republic, Latvia, Lebanon, Lesotho, Liberia, Libya, Liechtenstein, Lithuania, Luxembourg, Madagascar, Malawi, Malaysia, Maldives, Mali, Malta, Marshall Islands, Mauritania, Mauritius, Mexico, Micronesia (Federated States of), Monaco, Mongolia, Montenegro, Morocco, Mozambique, Myanmar, Namibia, Nauru, Nepal, Netherlands, New Zealand, Nicaragua, Niger, Nigeria, Niue, Norway, Oman, Pakistan, Palau, Palestine, Panama, Papua New Guinea, Paraguay, Peru, Philippines, Poland, Portugal, Qatar, Republic of Korea, Republic of Moldova, Romania, Russian Federation, Rwanda, Saint Kitts and Nevis, Saint Lucia, Saint Vincent and the Grenadines, Samoa, San Marino, Saudi Arabia, Senegal, Serbia, Seychelles, Sierra Leone, Singapore, Slovakia, Slovenia, Solomon Islands, Somalia, South Africa, Spain, Sri Lanka, Sudan, Suriname, Sweden, Switzerland, Syrian Arab Republic, Tajikistan, Thailand, The Former Yugoslav Republic of Macedonia, Timor-Leste, Togo, Tonga, Trinidad and Tobago, Tunisia, Turkey, Turkmenistan, Tuvalu, Uganda, Ukraine, United Arab Emirates, United Kingdom, United Republic of Tanzania, United States of America, Uruguay, Uzbekistan, Vanuatu, Venezuela, Vietnam, Yemen, Zambia, Zimbabwe

International organizations

African Union Commission, Association of Southeast Asian Nations, Boao Forum for Asia, Caribbean Community, Caribbean Development Bank, Common Market for Eastern and Southern Africa, Commonwealth of Independent States, European Organization for the Exploitation of Meteorological Satellites, European Union, Food and Agriculture Organization of the United Nations, Forum Francophone des Affaires, Global Environment Facility, Group on Earth Observations, International Association of Public Transport, International Atomic Energy Agency, International Council of Museums, International Development Information Network Association, International Energy Agency, International Federation of Red Cross and Red Crescent Societies, International Maritime Organization, International Network for Bamboo and Rattan, International Telecommunication Union, Joint United Nations Program on HIV/AIDS, League of Arab States, Organisation for Economic Cooperation and Development, Pacific Islands Forum, Convention on Biological Diversity, Shanghai Cooperation Organization, South Pacific Tourism Organization, UN Framework Convention on Climate Change, UN Habitat, World Organization of United Cities and Local Governments, United Nations, United Nations Capital Development Fund, United Nations Children's Fund, United Nations Conference on Trade and Development, United Nations Educational, Scientific and Cultural Organization, United Nations Environment Program, United Nations High Commissioner for Refugees, United Nations Industrial Development Organization, United Nations Population Fund, World Bank, World Health Organization, World Intellectual Property Organization, World Meteorological Organization, World Tourism Organization, World Trade Centers Association, World Trade Organization, World Water Council, World Wide Fund for Nature

EXPO

Contents

Pavilions in Zone C

EXPO

Exhibitions

E

D

A

B

C

N

W

E

S

黄浦江

世博轴

Theme
Pavilions

EXPO
2010

004

Expo 2010 has five theme pavilions, namely, Urbanian, City Being, Urban Planet, Footprint and Future.

They are the core pavilions in developing the theme "Better City, Better Life". By employing state-of-the-art exhibition technologies and in a visually compelling way, exhibitions in these pavilions show humanity, the city and the earth as an organic whole, and reveal the keys in bringing a better city and better life.

Urbanian Pavilion, Pavilion of City Being and Pavilion of Urban Planet are housed in the Theme Pavilion building in Zone B. Designers of the building, one of the Expo landmarks, have found inspiration in paper folding. As an attractive design feature, the roof imitates the dormer window that is often seen in Shikumen houses (an authentically Shanghai architectural style). The western exhibition hall, spanning 180 meters north-south and 126 meters east-west, does not use a single column. During the Expo, a wide range of events and ceremonies are held in the building's three squares.

The other two pavilions, Footprint and Future, are located in two modified industrial buildings in Zone D and Zone E respectively; they represent a careful consideration of environment protection and a fascinating mix of tradition and modernity.

上海
世博会

Urbanian Pavilion

Overall Human Development Is a Prerequisite for Sustainable Development of Cities

Zone **B**

Sustainable development of cities is possible only if we make urbanization a human-oriented process that promotes overall development of city dwellers. This is exactly why Urbanian Pavilion chooses human needs and development as its key thematic message. In its five thematic sections, i.e. Family, Work, Contact, Learning and Health, visitors will see the videos of six real families from six continents. The true stories of these city dwellers shed light on the macroscopic and microscopic relation between people and cities. Visitors will have a vivid view of city dwellers' life and the motivation behind the rural-to-urban shift.

In the Family section, mirrors mounted floor and ceiling provide visitors a window through which they can observe the lives of the six families. A gigantic machine, a metaphor of "factory, stock exchange and clock" is installed in the center of the Work Section. Besides the thematic sections, there is also a section named Diversified City where exhibits, settings and multimedia devices are combined to create 11 different city scenes.

006

Pavilion of City Being

The City, Like a Living Being, Needs the Protection of Humanity to Remain Healthy

Zone **B**

上海
世博会

The relationship between people and their cities is one of mutual benefit and dependence, and it gives rise to a living being in a brand new sense. In a metaphorical way, the Pavilion of City Being tries to depict the city as a living being with body and soul. Metabolism and circulation are important for it to function well. Constant adjustment between people and their cities is the key for the health of the city beings.

"Vigor Station" has five "kiosks" which represent population, logistics, energy, finance and information. The LCD display shows, on a real-time basis, the train, flight, ship, stock and foreign exchange information in the world's major cities. "Circulation System" leads visitors through vast underground pipes; and many interactive features in the section highlight the vulnerability of cities. The City Plaza section features movies about five world-renowned city plazas and provides a clue to the cultural identities of different cities. The "library" in the City Street section tries to use ten books to show how ten cities' rise and fall impacts the life of people.

Exhibitions
Theme Pavilions

Pavilion of Urban Planet

Theme

Humanity in Symbiosis with City and Planet

Zone **B**

EXPO 2010

The Earth, the planet housing both humanity and the cities they have created, is but an insignificant particle when compared to the infinite universe. With more and more people awakened and rising to urbanization and environmental challenges, a growing consensus is emerging that humanity is living in symbiosis with their city and planet. Through interesting exhibits, the Pavilion of Urban Planet enables visitors to understand cities as a source of both problems and solutions.

The exhibition space in the pavilion is in the form of two parallel spiral ramps. They are divided into five sections including Blue Planet and The Only Planet We Have, telling how the development, sometimes overdevelopment, of cities presents ecological problems. Blue Planet is a huge globe that represents the Earth. In a poetic way, it tells how cities, urban development and human behaviors impact the Earth. The Only Planet We Have is an interesting short movie about the interaction between cities, the Earth and people.

Pavilion of Footprint

Theme

Footprints Left as a Result of People's Interaction with Cities and the Environment from the Birth of the World's Cities to Modern Civilization

Zone D

History of cities, from their birth in remote antiquity to modern era, could always provide valuable insights. In a chorological order, the exhibitions in the pavilion, City's Origin, Growing City and Urban Wisdom, trace the birth and growth of cities, the challenges they face and the wisdom embodied in human responses.

The first exhibition hall City's Origin shows the formation of cities, including the origin of Chinese cities and the rise and fall of Greek city states. The second hall Growing City shows full-blown cities, including Florence, Amsterdam, cities in China's Song Dynasty and Japan's Edo Period. Urban Wisdom Hall deals with the Industrial Revolution era. Industrialization is depicted as a double-edged sword that changes the life in cities. New York and London are cited as examples of innovative wisdom in city planning and improvement of old town. The exhibition also shows the urban renewal efforts in Shanghai.

Pavilion of Future

Dream Inspires the Future of Cities

Zone
E

Dream could shape the future of an individual, and a city alike. The Pavilion of Future, built on the site of an industrial building, invites visitors to imagine what cities will be like in the future. It tells how a city was envisaged, planned and realized in history, and points to the fact that a future city relies on how we meet challenges today.

There are four exhibition sections, Dream of Yesterday, Dream and Practice, Future is Approaching and Multiple Possibilities. The exhibitions start with a depiction of future cities. Through movies, books and sculptures, they propose various possibilities of a future city, and point to the spiritual elements that have always driven human progress. The displays in the Future Is Approaching section focus on intelligent home, healthy community, low-carbon city and harmonious environment and help visitors to better understand the trend of technological advancement.

Zone A

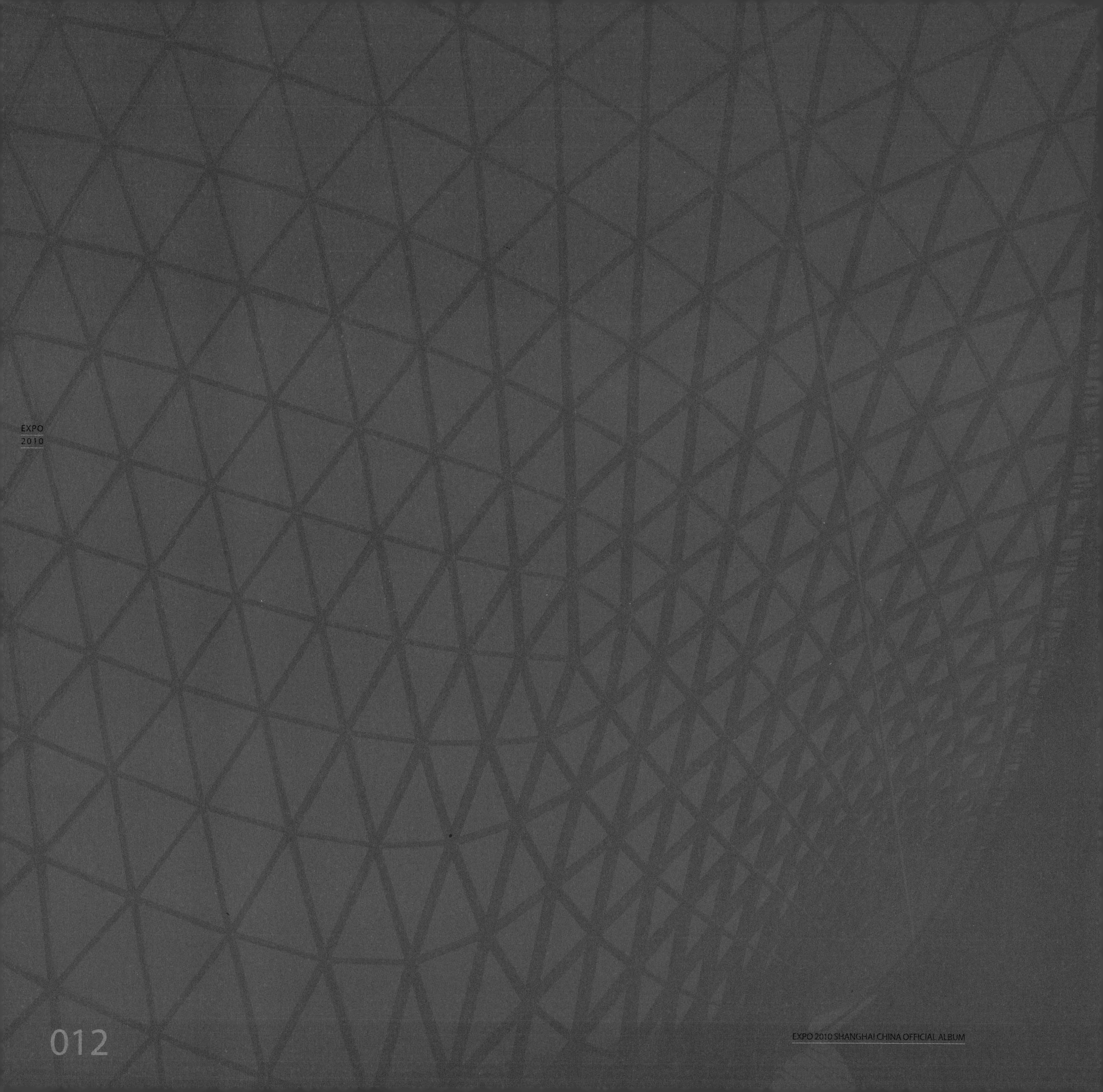

EXPO
2010

China Pavilion

Chinese Wisdom in Urban Development

Zone	National Day	Year	Month	Day
A		2010	10	1

Themed on "Oriental Crown, Splendid China, Ample Barn, Rich People", the pavilion tries to reveal an ideal that is deep-rooted in Chinese culture.

Consisting of The Footprint, The Dialogue and The Actions sections, China Pavilion's exhibitions will take visitors on a journey of quest, encouraging them to discover and comprehend on the Chinese wisdom in evolution of cities. Starting with the country's unparalleled urbanization achievements over the past three decades, the exhibitions seek to shed light on the classical wisdom embodied in China's urban development process. Then visitors are invited to ponder over the future, over an urban development path illuminated by the Chinese values and development outlook.

Section 1: In The Footprint section, a short movie tells the experience of Chinese in urbanization over the past three decades, their passion for construction and faith

上海
世博会

Exhibitions
Zone A

013

in a bright future; then, a celebrated painting *Along the River during the Qingming Festival* is displayed to reflect the ancient Chinese wisdom about cities.

Section 2: This section features a ride themed as a "dialogue between past and present". It offers a dynamic and exciting tour of discovery, enabling the visitors to find out themselves about the Chinese wisdom in city planning.

Section 3: The exhibition focuses on a low-carbon lifestyle that will shape the development of Chinese cities in the future. It shows how Chinese are inspired by nature and propose their own solutions to global challenges in urbanization and sustainable development.

Asia Joint Pavilion I

The joint pavilion encompasses the exhibitions of Bangladesh, Kyrgyzstan, Maldives, Mongolia, Tajikistan and Timor-Leste.

上海
世博会

Bangladesh Pavilion

Spirit and Growth of Golden Bengal

Zone	National Day	Year	Month	Day
A		2010	9	20

The unconquerable people of Bangladesh have always been the source and drive for the country's development. Bangladesh has made great progress in clothing, jute, tea, fishery, leather, crafts, shipbuilding and pharmacy. The pavilion aims to showcase the image, intelligence and potential of the country.

The pavilion entrance is decorated with colorful traditional Bangladeshi patterns. A small sculpture, pictures of new urban areas, and models of traditional architecture in the pavilion symbolize the dialogue between tradition and future. Pictures on a wall show the Bangladeshi features, and a catering area provides Bangladeshi food.

Kyrgyzstan Pavilion

Theme

Bishkek — the City Open to the World

Zone	National Day	Year	Month	Day
A		2010	8	4

The pavilion, resembling a yurt, symbolizes the harmonious coexistence of the nomadic people and nature. The pavilion stresses harmony of capital Bishkek which is a famous city in Central Asia with a time-honored history. Though highly industrial, it is a liveable city with large green area. The development of satellite cities around it embodies the interaction between harmonious urban development and environmental protection.

The three sections in the pavilion present the unique characteristics of the country and Bishkek from different perspectives. Movies, posters, slides, real objects and cultural activities introduce the country's culture, history and customs, and the harmonious development of economy, culture and tourism in Bishkek.

上海
世博会

Maldives Pavilion

In the past decade, diversified tourism and fishery have become the pillars of Maldives' urban development. The pavilion describes the country's efforts in socioeconomic transition, social harmony and economic prosperity. Beside, Maldives maintains a simple and natural lifestyle while inheriting culture and protecting the environment.

Various methods are applied to present the country's lifestyle, art, tourism, fishery and urbanization process. Distinctive setting and a variety of exhibits unfold its natural scenery and folk culture. Besides, the exhibited seafood demonstrates the country's rich fishery resources.

Mongolia Pavilion

Theme
Gobi and the City

Zone	National Day	Year	Month	Day
A		2010	9	13

Used to be a land-locked sea in ancient times, Gobi boasts numerous dinosaur skeletons, dinosaur egg fossils and mineral resources. However, its fragile natural environment impedes modern urban development. The exhibited huge dinosaur egg, symbolizing the fragile city, implies that urban development must be based on ecological balance.

A huge dinosaur egg and two dinosaur skeleton models in it make visitors imagine the mysterious ancient times. Besides, models of baby dinosaurs and wooden tents convey the importance of environmental protection.

上海
世博会

Tajikistan Pavilion

Theme

The Evolution of City Structure and the Good Life

Zone	National Day	Year	Month	Day
A		2010	9	22

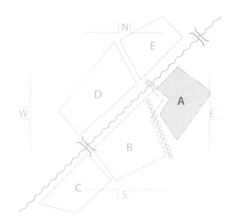

Early in the Silk Road period, Tajikistan had already played an important role in the West-East communication in economy, trade, and culture as well as dialogues between different civilizations. The country is rich in hydropower resources and mountains, which is reflected in the pavilion through simulated snow-capped mountains and waterfalls as is in real natural environment.

Models of historical events and architectures are used to depict work and life of people in such a mountainous country. Abundant photos present Tajikistan's typical artworks, recent achievements in urban construction and its friendship with neighboring countries.

EXPO 2010

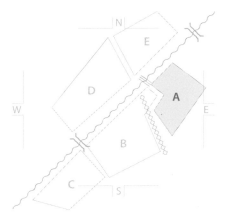

Timor-Leste Pavilion

Theme

Be with Us, Be with Nature

Zone	National Day	Year	Month	Day
A		2010	7	13

Timor-Leste boasts abundant natural resources and charming sceneries. Lospalos-style roof, carved wooden door, processed palm leaves and a dazzling array of handicrafts depict a unique look of the country. The exhibition stresses sustainable urban development and the harmonious coexistence of humanity and nature.

With the help of lighting, the country's natural scenery, scenes of work and entertainment of its people are displayed. A day from dawn to dusk in the country shows people's tranquil and leisure life. Besides, various handicrafts such as wood and stone carvings are exhibited. Visitors will also feast their eyes and ears on local songs and dances.

上海
世博会

Asia Joint Pavilion II

The joint pavilion has the exhibitions of Afghanistan, Bahrain, Jorden, Palestine, Syria and Yemen.

EXPO
2010

Afghanistan Pavilion

Theme

Afghanistan — Heart of Asia, Land of Opportunities & Resources

Zone	National Day	Year	Month	Day
A		2010	8	19

上海
世博会

Located in Central Asia, Afghanistan boasts rich cultural heritage and a time-honoured history. Trade and exchanges at the border area of Eurasia have promoted the integration of diverse culture in the country.

The pavilion is a reconstruction of the famous Blue Mosque of Herat. The rich blue and green mosaic tiles take visitors right into the stories of the *Oriental Nights* and attract them to move inside where unique products and handicrafts are exhibited. The Rahimy Collection of Afghan Treasures present more than 400 unique exhibits. The nomad tent, Kilim rugs, textiles, objects of daily life, traditional silver jewellery and corals are surely to dazzle visitors. The bazaar inside the pavilion sells handicrafts, nuts and dry fruits, jewellery, textiles, spices and herbs, etc.

Bahrain Pavilion

Theme
Small Is Beautiful

Zone	National Day	Year	Month	Day
A		2010	10	22

Bahrain is a beautiful country in Persian Gulf, A Pearl of the Gulf always in spring. It has a long history and profound culture, and serves as a trade center in the Gulf with great tolerance and global perspective. Bahrain people enjoy cozy urban life brought by developed finance, abundant oil resources and rich cultural activities. The pavilion is a classical architecture with a white exterior wall and curves are applied in the design of internal structure, such as the curved path.

Replicas of cultural relics with high archeological value, Bahrain jewelries and videos showcase the history, culture and folk customs of the country. Touch-screen interactions bring visitors close to Bahrain's unique way of living and national heritage and interpret its theme "Small is Beautiful".

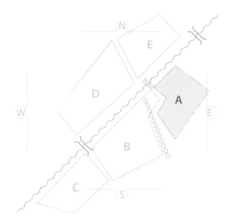

Jordan Pavilion

Theme

"We are CITY… We are LIFE"
We Make Our Ordinary
Lifestyle, Extraordinary!!

Zone	National Day	Year	Month	Day
A		2010	7	25

Jordan is a melting pot of cultures where people are working hard to build cities for a better future. The pavilion presents the charm of ancient civilization, interprets the harmony between human, cities, nature and life, and delivers the idea about everlasting development and renovation in the past, at present and in the future.

Entrance of the pavilion resembles architectures in ancient Petra. The pavilion houses magnificent Khazneh, a grand architecture of Hellenistic style with the legend of *Ali Baba and the Forty Thieves*. Also displayed are the evolution of Aqaba from a port to a city of commerce and leisure as well as ways of living and innovation in other cities.

上海
世博会

Palestine Pavilion

Theme
Olive City Peace City

Zone	National Day	Year	Month	Day
A		2010	10	16

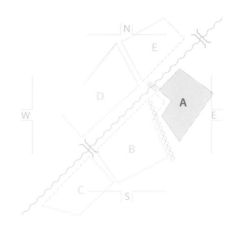

Olive is important to Palestine as olive oil is the country's major economic crop. Olive branch signifies peace and friendship, and olive green symbolizes harmony, environmental protection and sustainable development. The pavilion presents a fantastic City of Olive with a facade featuring Palestine flag and a solemn Arabic gate. In the center erects a huge olive with visual impact. The exhibition gives an insight of Palestine's cultural, geographical and economical charms.

Multimedia screens and embedded lanterns display abundant products and distinctive culture of the country, traditional Islamic painting, language and civilization, as well as Palestinian people's wishes for freedom and better future.

Syria Pavilion

Theme

Damascus: the Oldest Capital Still Inhabited

Zone	National Day	Year	Month	Day
A		2010	10	17

As one of the cradles of human civilization, Syria boasts rich history and culture, and is still inhabited by people of various religions and cultures. In the pavilion, the thousands of years' history and harmony of Damascus, the capital of Syria, as well as distinctive architecture and culture of Syria is well interpreted by traditional elements—folk residences in Damascus as embodied in architectures and three stories.

Three components of the exhibition, Cultural Stories of the Wheat/Silk Road, Arabic Library, and From Ancient Hamoukar to Modern Damascus, are respectively arranged in three rooms dwelled by three generations and linked with each other. In the courtyard there is a well in the center, valuable antiques around, and aromatic bonsais in the corners.

上海
世博会

Yemen Pavilion

Theme
Yemen: Art and Civilization

Zone	National Day	Year	Month	Day
A		2010	10	14

EXPO
2010

Yemen boasts a long history and unsophisticated people. The pavilion presents Yemen's major achievements in culture, tourism and science, stressing the importance of economy and trade in urban development. Sanaa, the capital of Yemen, is an open museum, has unique architectures and beautiful landscape.

Multiple means are used to display Yemen's experience in industrial development and practices in trade of various types, and envision its economic and trade development. A City Model brings scenes of modern city in Yemen; posters with Arabic, English and Chinese captions introduce historical cities, renovated villages and natural landscape. Handicrafts and industrial products are sold in the pavilion.

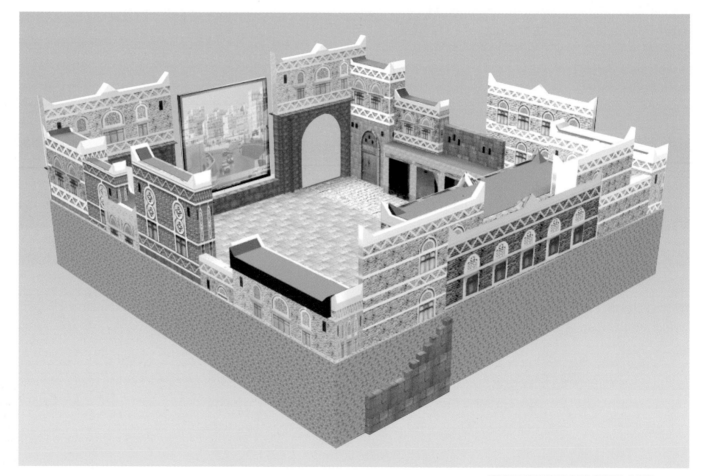

EXPO 2010 SHANGHAI CHINA OFFICIAL ALBUM

Asia Joint Pavilion III

The joint pavilion encompasses the exhibitions of Laos and Myanmar.

上海
世博会

Laos Pavilion

Theme

City of Charm — Luang Prabang
Charming World Heritage Town

Zone	National Day	Year	Month	Day
A		2010	10	12

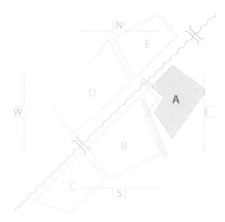

Laos attracts the world people with its rolling hills, dense forests, natural sceneries and unique customs. The model of Luang Prabang, an ancient city which has been inscribed on the World Heritage List, together with other exhibits, highlights the connection between tradition and the modern society, the integration of heritage preservation and tourism development, the interrelation between environmental protection and economic prosperity and the importance of sustainable urban development.

The unique lamps and lanterns, textiles, handicrafts and traditional dances reflect the local customs of Laos. Posters and pictures show natural sceneries such as hills, waterfalls and caves and local buildings.

Myanmar Pavilion

Myanmar boasts rich species, beautiful landscape and numerous historical sites. The pavilion-style entrance, magnificent wall, the bridge, and other symmetrical and bright-color structures represent distinct Southeast Asian flavor and the charming architectural style of Myanmar.

Featuring holy temples and traditional buildings, the pavilion adopts advanced display methods to introduce local customs, rich resources and brilliant culture of Myanmar, and to outline the prospect of its eco-friendly urbanization. A large number of local products and handicrafts are also exhibited.

上海
世博会

Chinese Provinces Joint Pavilion

Zone **A**

Like a solid platform, Chinese Provinces Joint Pavilion surrounds China Pavilion which rises at the center.

A total of 31 provinces, autonomous regions and municipalities stage their exhibitions here. They can explore the Expo theme Better City, Better Life from their own perspectives and exhibit their cultural features, city landscapes and yearning for a better urban life.

Beijing Pavilion

Theme

Charming Capital:
Culture, Technology and
Environment-Friendliness

Zone	Theme Week	Year	Month	Day
A		2010	5	4~8

No single image can fully capture the immense charm of Beijing, as one of the attractions of the capital city is the dynamic changes taking place every day. That is exactly why the designers decided to make the Beijing Pavilion a building that can transform its shape into the Temple of Heaven at one moment, into Water Cube, NCPA, and the Bird's Nest. Within the wonderful pavilion, visitors may know more about the many Hutong (lanes) that dot the city's landscape, watch the real-time images of the Chang'an Street, or enjoy an exciting short movie directed by Zhang Yimou.

Tianjin Pavilion

Theme

The Exciting and Charming Binhai District: Eco-Friendly

Zone	Theme Week	Year	Month	Day
A		2010	5	9~13

The pavilion design draws inspiration from a typical western-style building in Tianjin, in an attempt to highlight the integration of Chinese and western cultures and a fascinating mix of international architectural styles that characterizes the city. A high-speed train car, which is actually a small cinema, will be put on display in the pavilion. There will be exhibitions showing the city's unique customs and culture.

上海
世博会

Hebei Pavilion

Theme

Charming Hebei, Beijing's Garden

Zone	Theme Week	Year	Month	Day
A		2010	5	14~18

The pavilion features five interconnected geometric structures surrounded by a huge glass wall. The design is inspired by the province's art of interior painting. The five buildings, like strands of DNA, form an integral "living being". They symbolize the geographic proximity and close cultural ties between Hebei and Beijing. The Chinese philosophy about integration and symbiosis runs through the exhibitions in the pavilion which trace the history, cultural and aesthetic traditions of the province, and look into the future.

Shanxi Pavilion

Theme

Era of Power Development

Zone	Theme Week	Year	Month	Day
A		2010	5	19~23

A magnificent archway stands as the centerpiece of the pavilion design. Powdered coal bricks, the environment-friendly building material, and LED lights are used for exterior walls which will show the images of the province's world cultural heritage sites, intangible cultural heritage and folk art and traditions.

The exhibitions in the pavilion provide a full picture of local culture, competence in energy technologies and vision for the future.

Inner Mongolia Pavilion

Theme

Prairie Civilization in Urban Development

Zone	Theme Week	Year	Month	Day
A		2010	5	24~28

The pavilion depicts a prairie civilization in urban development and manifests various elements of the prairie culture with unique exhibition items. The floor, consisting of three kinds of sand, manifests the Inner Mongolian people's wisdom; the contrast between the earliest nomadic habitation and modern cities shows the course of prairie city development; the huge tree of quicksand implies environmental changes and expresses the ideal of turning deserts into oases. Visitors can also have a virtual prairie journey on mountain bikes.

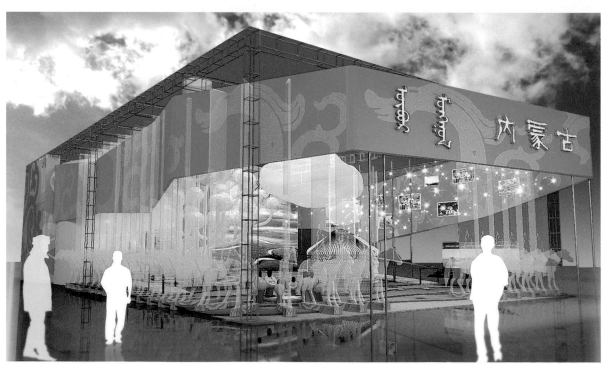

Liaoning Pavilion

Theme

Liaoning: Rhythm of Steel and Sea

Zone	Theme Week	Year	Duration
A		2010	5.29~6.2

The pavilion's blue metal exterior, full of rhythm, manifests the hardness of steel and the beauty of the sea. Above the entrance is a Sinosauropteryx model. The exhibits include the fossils of the first bird and flower in the world, Liaoning's six world cultural heritage items and its 200 greatest contributions to China's economy; the 4D cinema with a 360° screen introduces the Liaoning coastal economic belt and Shenyang economic zone; multimedia movies show the charm of 14 Liaoning cities.

上海
世博会

Jilin Pavilion

Theme

Sing Under Changbai Mountains

Zone	Theme Week	Year	Month	Day
A		2010	6	3~7

The exterior design incorporates such visual elements as Tianchi Lake of Changbai Mountains, forests and alpine gardens to exhibit the unique landscape of the province and its green city ideal. Exhibitions and activities within the pavilion include interactive videos on forests, environment-friendly car assembly, train driving, and Changbai Mountain Tour in a 4D cinema.

Heilongjiang Pavilion

Theme

Ice and Snow Makes us Different

Zone	Theme Week	Year	Month	Day
A		2010	6	8~12

The pavilion, made of crystal resin, is in the shape of an ice sculpture. Focusing on ice and snow, it displays Heilongjiang's green tourist culture and showcases its people's happy life. The interior, featuring ice, snow, water-eroded cave and other elements, makes visitors feel cool and comfortable. Visitors can see panoramic movies and folk performances on simulated sleds and participate in interactive games such as curling and skiing.

Jiangsu Pavilion

Theme

Beautiful Jiangsu, Wonderful Home

Zone	Theme Week	Year	Month	Day
A		2010	6	13~17

The pavilion creates a virtual garden through many high-tech means. The exterior consists of two LED screens, showing Jiangsu's openness and vitality. Main exhibition items such as Spring Flowers and Autumn Fruits, Internet of Things Seven-colored Spectrum and Beautiful Jiangsu fully showcase Jiangsu's long history and profound culture. The development achievements of the high-tech industry represented by the Internet of things, photovoltaic and biological medicine display the essence of an ideal garden.

Zhejiang Pavilion

Theme

Urban and Rural Happiness, Wonderful Home

Zone	Theme Week	Year	Month	Day
A		2010	6	18~22

The pavilion's main exhibition item is designed as a huge celadon bowl brimming over with water. The scenes of the West Lake and Qiantang River Tide are projected onto the center of the huge bowl. The four sections of High Mountains and Winding Rivers, Like a Heavenly City. Dazzling Stars and Rippling Water show Zhejiang's urbanization mode characterized by overall urban and rural planning.

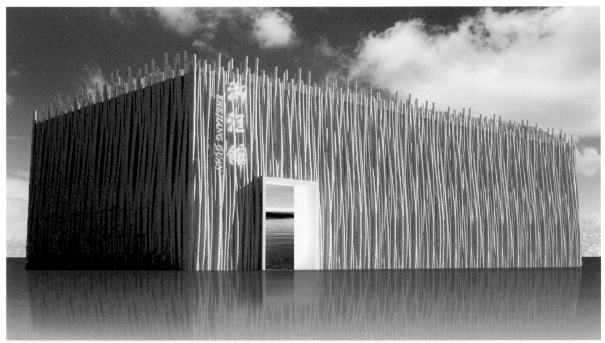

上海
世博会

Anhui Pavilion

Theme

Hui Culture Lends Greater Charm to Life — Essential to Cities

Zone	Theme Week	Year	Month	Day
A		2010	6	23~27

The pavilion focuses on the Hui culture's core idea of "openness, ambition, innovation, harmony and good faith" in urban development. The two sections of Anhui Impression and Colorful Cities depict a panoramic picture of Anhui's past, present and future. Anhui Impression shows calligraphic works and Anhui residences; Colorful Cities is a multimedia presentation displaying beautiful sceneries in the province.

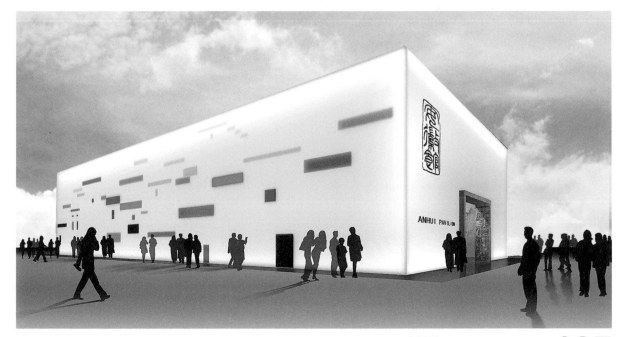

Fujian Pavilion

Theme

Magic Fujian—a Land of Promise

Zone	Theme Week	Year	Duration
A		2010	6.28~7.2

The boat-shaped pavilion with green, blue and white as main colors fully shows the charming image of Fujian as a livable place. Exhibits and multimedia presentation together showcase natural sceneries in Fujian as well as its achievements in socioeconomic development, technology and urban construction.

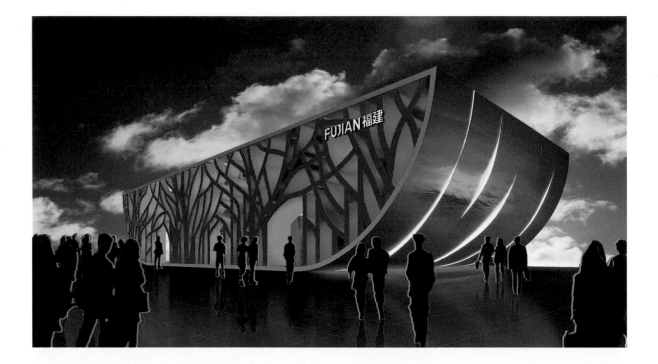

Jiangxi Pavilion

Theme

Jiangxi: EcoProvince

Zone	Theme Week	Year	Month	Day
A		2010	7	3~7

The pavilion, resembling a huge blue and white porcelain container, depicts the peculiar charm of Jiangxi as home to a myriad of talents and natural resources. The exhibition presents Jiangxi's splendid scenery, profound culture and current development. The plan for the Poyang Lake Ecological Economic Zone shows that Jiangxi is pursuing sustainable development and harmony between humanity and nature.

Shandong Pavilion

Theme
A Lush, Green Garden

Zone	Theme Week	Year	Month	Day
A		2010	7	8~12

The pavilion embodies the cultural conception of "stretching mountains and rivers" and depicts Shandong's geographical features from the main perspective of the towering Mt. Tai. The open entrance displays the hospitality for friends from afar. The three sections of Wisdom Corridor, City Window and Shandong Home show Shandong's culture, charm, hospitality and future city life and interpret the idea of "Harmonious but Different, Our Home".

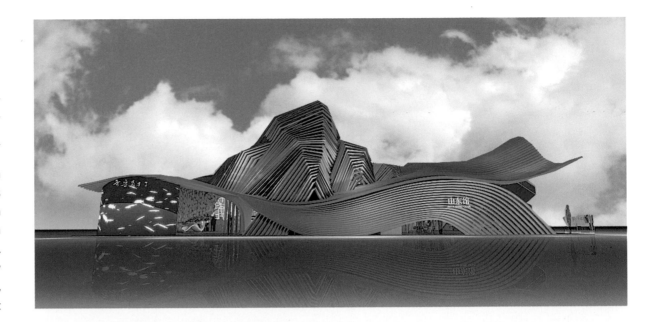

Henan Pavilion

Theme
Heart of the Nation, Origin of Urban Civilization

Zone	Theme Week	Year	Month	Day
A		2010	7	13~17

The pavilion enumerates Henan's contributions to and impacts on the Chinese civilization, manifests the inspiration and stimulation of historical achievements for future development and envisions the harmonious future of Henan cities. It displays the long historical course of urban development. A movie on the provincial history is played in the theme cinema area, looking to the province's wonderful future.

Hubei Pavilion

Theme

Rivers, Gardens
Passion for Life

Zone	Theme Week	Year	Month	Day
A		2010	7	18~22

The pavilion in the shape of the Chinese character for "water" is decorated by a phoenix pattern, a symbol unique to Hubei. It has wonderful exhibition space. Its pavilion embodies the urban development course, wonderful visions and the idea of harmony between cities and water. The main exhibition item sets forth the idea that history of water is the urban history and mankind's history through the integrated panorama screen, yarn screen and 3D ground screen system.

Hunan Pavilion

Theme

Urban Shangri-La

Zone	Theme Week	Year	Month	Day
A		2010	7	23~27

The pavilion looks like a Möbius strip. The review of Hunan's history and vision of future projected on the strip imply man's endless pursuit. Among sections named Nature, Future and Human Culture, the first two show the local scenery and imagine future cities — a "urban Shangri-La" featuring ecological soundness, pleasant environment, energy recycling and sustainable development; the remaining one allows children to think freely about future cities in games.

Guangdong Pavilion

Theme

Guangdong Qilou, Green Life

Zone	Theme Week	Year	Duration
A		2010	7.28~8.1

The pavilion in the shape of Qilou (special local structure) draws on local paper cutting techniques to demonstrate the strong Guangdong taste. The three sections of Green Life, Green Cities and Green Myths interpret the pursuit of green life through high-tech means and ingenious thoughts. The green myths interpreted by special-effect movies are amazing and touching; "Brightening the Whole of Heaven" shows Guangdong's beautiful green life via 3D presentation, performances and shows.

上海
世博会

Guangxi Pavilion

Theme

Green Home, Blue Dream

Zone	Theme Week	Year	Month	Day
A		2010	8	2~6

With the Elephant Trunk Mountain covered by osmanthus blossoms as visual framework, the pavilion shows the beautiful landscape of the province. Robots dressed in Zhuang style greet visitors at the entrance. The theme is demonstrated through various means to show local customs. The bronze drum image and phantom silk ball are of particular charms.

Hainan Pavilion

Theme

Hainan: Where You Experience a Better Life

Zone	Theme Week	Year	Month	Day
A		2010	8	7~11

Focusing on "vacation paradise, habitable island, open special zone", the pavilion looks magic and romantic by combining advanced digital projection technologies with wonderful silk screen designs, and make people feel Hainan's sunshine, leisure, livability, security and other charms.

Chongqing Pavilion

Theme

Mountains and Forest City

Zone	Theme Week	Year	Month	Day
A		2010	8	12~16

The shape of the pavilion borrows the elements of Kuimen and steep mountains, highlighting the pattern of "a mountain city surrounded by two rivers". The three sections and the two interaction areas interpret the city's changes by presenting the city's footprints of ecological, cultural and urban development. The pavilion shows Chongqing's new mode of economic growth and the vision of mountain and forest city from aspects of Habitable Chonging, Forest Chongqing, and Healthy Chongqing.

Sichuan Pavilion

Theme
Water: Lifeline of Sichuan

Zone	Theme Week	Year	Month	Day
A		2010	8	17~21

The two-layer structure is based on the special landscape of Sichuan. The internal circular wall with projected ecological images is surrounded by the external one with a hyperboloid structure, embodying the harmonious coexistence of cities and nature. The history and culture of Jinsha Sunbird lead visitors into a secluded, beautiful and harmonious world. The three sections display Sichuan's urban history and civilization, the wisdom of "following the law of nature" and wonderful future.

上海
世博会

Guizhou Pavilion

Theme
Guizhou: Intoxicating Beauty of a Summer Paradise

Zone	Theme Week	Year	Month	Day
A		2010	8	22~26

The pavilion's grand and magnificent appearance is a combination of unique visual elements of Guizhou, such as wind and rain bridge, drum tower, etc. The architectural shape boldly exaggerates the form of ethnic minorities' silver head decorations, displaying special folk characteristics. The pavilion shows the intoxicating beauty of local ecological environment and folk customs and blueprints a network city featuring harmony between man and nature.

Yunnan Pavilion

Theme

Diverse Beauty of Yunnan: Rural-Urban Harmony

Zone	Theme Week	Year	Month	Day
A		2010	8	27~31

On an open, spacious and distinctive square, Yunnan Pavilion revivifies national architectures such as Golden Horse Archway, the Bai people's residence and the Dai bamboo house, and integrates local elements like Ox-tiger Bronze Table and purple pottery from Jianshui. It presents the local "six-tier" urban system and achievements of new rural construction, and exhibits the beautiful scenery, colorful folk culture and harmonious urban-rural development on different themes via multimedia.

Tibet Pavilion

Theme

Roof of World

Zone	Theme Week	Year	Month	Day
A		2010	9	1~5

Concentrating on "New Tibet, Better Life" and taking "Environmental Protection, Folk Cultural Inheritance and Sustainable Development" as the exhibition idea, Tibet Pavilion displays the unique charms of Tibetan culture, Tibetan people's patriotism, resolution to make progress, and aspiration for well-off life, peace and harmony through exhibited items like Qinghai-Tibet Railway, Housing Project, multimedia interactive streets and short videos.

Shaanxi Pavilion

Theme
A Cultural Trip to Chang'an

Zone	Theme Week	Year	Month	Day
A		2010	9	6~10

The pavilion takes the form of Tang-style palaces and presents the living scenes of the royal family in the past and ordinary people at present by mainly depicting the Huaqing Hot Spring, Huaqing Palace and the story in *Song of Everlasting Sorrow*. Exhibitions on four themes are held to display the splendid culture, modern urban life and natural beauty of the province through interaction between robots and visitors as well as wonderful folk shows and Tang-style performances.

上海
世博会

Gansu Pavilion

Theme
Silk Road, Song of Cities

Zone	Theme Week	Year	Month	Day
A		2010	9	11~15

Gansu Pavilion, employing LED light kit and revivified models in its exterior, demonstrates the glorious culture of Gansu Province through artistic elements of world-renowned Dunhuang Grottoes. The exhibition displays the vicissitudes and revival of cities along the Silk Road on three themes, and highlights Dunhuang's history and culture, emerging urban civilization represented by the urban construction achievements since the founding of the PRC and sustainable development concept embodied in circular economy.

Qinghai Pavilion

Theme

Source of Three Great Rivers: Watering the Nation

Zone	Theme Week	Year	Month	Day
A		2010	9	16~20

Qinghai Pavilion demonstrates how the Yantze River, the Yellow River and the Lancang River originating from Qinghai have nurtured riverfront cities and civilization, and reveals the supportive and restrictive role of the ecological conditions at the source of the three great rivers in urban development.

Over ten exhibition items shed light on the public ecological concept, reflect the subsistance-development relation, and rest people's hope for ecological civilization.

Ningxia Pavilion

Theme

Natural Ningxia, Harmonious Land

Zone	Theme Week	Year	Month	Day
A		2010	9	21~25

Lumpy curves and the distinctive structure symbolize the diverse landscapes and the integration of various cultures in Ningxia Province. Bearing the Islamic style, the pavilion holds exhibitions on different themes to mainly display the economic development, technical progress and culture of cities along the Yellow River, reflecting the fertility and beauty of the province at the heart of the river basin and presenting an open, harmonious and vigorous Ningxia.

Xinjiang Pavilion

Theme
Xinjiang is a Nice Place

Zone	Theme Week	Year	Month	Day
A		2010	9	26~30

The pavilion's exterior walls incorporate Xinjiang architectural elements and cultural symbols to achieve a perfect color collocation and create romantic artistic atmosphere. The curved lines imply the dancing silk. Themed as "Xinjiang is a Nice Place", the pavilion, divided into three sections, demonstrates the generosity and cheerfulness of Xinjiang people.

Shanghai Pavilion

Theme
New Horizons Forever

Zone	Theme Week	Year	Month	Day
A		2010	10	8~12

Taking the form of Shikumen, Shanghai Pavilion features simple design but deep implication, plain appearance but modern taste, perfectly matching the city's characteristics of combination of decency and diversity, blending of history and modernism, and meeting of the East and the West. Themed as "New Horizons Forever", it demonstrates a more charming, harmonious and intelligent Shanghai through the exterior wall, waiting room and interior space.

Democratic People's Republic of Korea Pavilion

Theme
Paradise of People

Zone	National Day	Year	Month	Day
A		2010	9	6

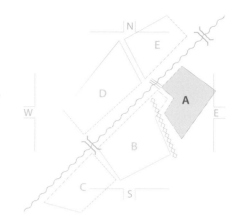

The pavilion combines traditional features and modern beauty, and adopts patterns of national flag and bronze statue of horse to decorate the exterior wall. A river winds through the exhibition hall, symbolizing the River Taedong.

Exhibition items such as Tower of Juche Idea, River Taedong and Korean-style arbour show Pyongyang's beautiful scenery and great achievements in education, science, culture, sports, etc. A section of national customs and a small cave are set to reproduce a world heritage item and display local paintings.

Hong Kong Pavilion

Hong Kong: the Infinite City

Zone
A

The three-storey pavilion, with the storey in the middle transparent, reflects the modern, open and promising city, and showcases its close relationship with the world in terms of transport, information and finance.

A miniature wetland park is set on the 3rd floor. The roofless open space guarantees sufficient sunshine and rainwater for the plants. Art exhibitions are held to introduce the development of ink-and-wash painting and the city's unique culture integrating Chinese and Western elements.

上海
世博会

Exhibitions
Zone A

049

India Pavilion

Theme
Cities of Harmony

Zone	National Day	Year	Month	Day
A		2010	8	18

The India Pavilion exemplifies India's rich cultural heritage, its diversity of faith, traditional and modern scientific & technological development and urban–rural integration so as to present the theme "Cities of Harmony". The pavilion's design draws inspirations from Indian's great buildings such as Siddi Syed Temple and Sanchi Stupa. Zero-chemical substances characterises the pavilion due to the use of solar panels, wind power, herbs and bamboos.

Indian characteristics are displayed in multimedia movies, cultural shows, delicacies, and specialized products. Visitors are led to a journey of Indian cities to experience the life in ancient, middle-age and modern India, and learn about the interaction between tradition and modernity as well as the harmonious living of different sections of society in rural and urban areas. Exhibition on creative design and cutting-edge technology is worth visiting.

Iran Pavilion

As main design elements for the pavilion, water stands for universe, soil for humanity and creation, light for nature and source of divine spirit, and colors for various species. They depict the grandeur of ancient and modern Iranian art. Referring to a local 36-arch bridge, the pavilion adopts arch decorations on the four elevations, LED screen on the north, and genuine paintings on the west. Ancient-style gate and interior decoration remind people of the architectural style of Isfahan.

The exhibition hall is divided into three parts concerning the history of ethnic groups and civilizations, Islamic architecture and cultural achievements. Intelligent robots, advanced technologies and musical entertainment facilities are also shown.

Israel Pavilion

Innovation for Life: Dialog with Nature History, and Future Needs

Zone	National Day	Year	Month	Day
A		2010	5	6

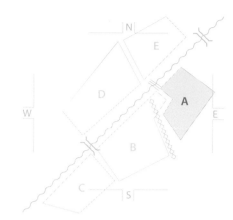

The Israel Pavilion is an innovative and futuristic structure. The pavilion consists of two streamline buildings that resemble two clenching hands and a sea shell.

There are three experience areas: Whispering Garden, Hall of Light and Hall of Innovation. Whispering Garden has a quiet, tranquil and welcoming environment. The orchard has 54 orange trees, displaying Israel's drip irrigation technology and agricultural characteristics. The Hall of Light is covered in PVC glass symbolizing technology, transparency, light and the future; it presents Israel's culture, landscape and history. The Hall of Innovation is set up in natural stone symbolizing the connection to earth and history. Inside the hall awaits the high point of the tour: a floated sphere in 3D space presents 360° audiovisual performances about Israel's technological innovations to improve human life. These discoveries include diesel oil extraction from plants for aviation use; intelligent "horseshoes" to read the minds of the cows, a "capsule"—a mini camera, which could be swallowed for photography and offer a pain-free physical examination.

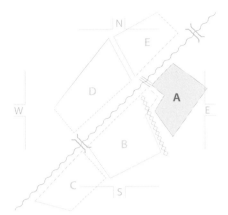

Japan Pavilion

Theme

Wa: Harmony of Hearts, Harmony of Arts

Zone	National Day	Year	Month	Day
A		2010	6	12

Know as Purple Silkworm Island, the pavilion is covered with a super-light membrane with solar cells, which adopts special environmental technology enabling it to be a "breathing organism" and "environment-friendly architechture". By virtual reproduction and imaging technique, the pavilion envisions the urban life of 2020 and introduces the cultural relationship between China and Japan in history, the co-existence of Nature and high-tech devices developed for resolving depletion of water resources and global environmental issues. In the pavilion, both the warm-up show set in a mountain village and the theme performance presented in a traditional Japanese wooden theatre are themed on Sino-Japanese cooperation on protection of crested ibis, a kind of rare bird. For the warm-up show, the world's top robots will make their debut ; For the theme performance, the musical co-starred by actors from China and Japan will be a crystal of Kun, a traditional Chinese opera, and Noh, a traditional Japanese opera.

上海
世博会

Kazakhstan Pavilion

Theme
Astana — the Heart of Eurasia

Zone	National Day	Year	Month	Day
A		2010	6	5

The pavilion is designed to show the charm of the dynamically developing capital Astana, a shining pearl along the Silk Road, in economy, education, medicine, and culture. Drawing inspiration from the tents of the nomadic people in its shape, the pavilion features stretched membrane and glass curtain wall, characteristic of Kazakhstan's modern architecture. The interior design in the central hall reflects the integration between tradition and modernity.

The pavilion consists of 8 exhibition areas: Territory of Knowledge, 4D Cinema, Urban Matrix 2030, Interactive Entertainments, Area of Astana, Soft Tribune, Art-Zone (photo gallery) and Farewell to Kazakhstan, showing Astana's history and future by multimedia and advanced information systems.

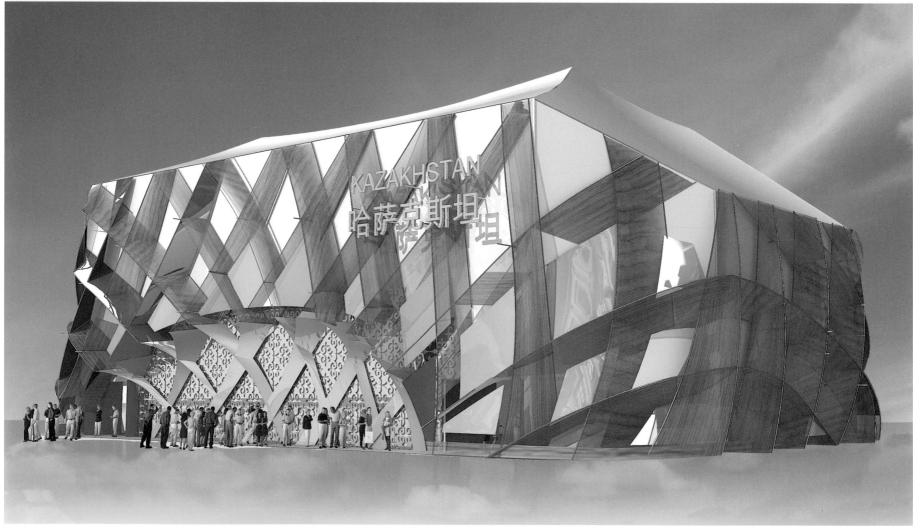

Lebanon Pavilion

Lebanon, a hub of communication between the East and the West, witnesses the development of international trade and human history. The pavilion tells stories about the progress of ancient cities and explains the role of cultures and religions in the process from perspectives of local customs, natural resources, and environmental protection.

The pavilion helps visitors understand how traditional cultures have pushed Lebanon's development. On display is the Phoenician writing on the Ahiram sarcophagus, which is widely considered to be the origin of Hebrew, Greek and Latin. Jeita Grotto, one of the country's natural wonders, is presented in multimedia form.

上海
世博会

Macao Pavilion

Theme
Spirit of Cultures, Essence of Harmony

Zone
A

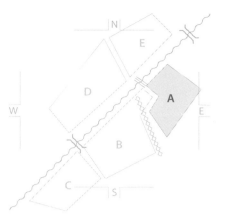

The pavilion, in the shape of a jade rabbit lantern popular in south China, is 19.99m high, implying the year of Macao's return to China. The pavilion is wrapped with a double-layer glass membrane and features fluorescent screens on its exterior wall. Two balloons, as head and tail of the "rabbit", can move up and down.

Entering the pavilion, there is a circular screen along the spiral ramp, making visitors feel like walking in a time tunnel. A movie about Macao's local customs and history is screened.

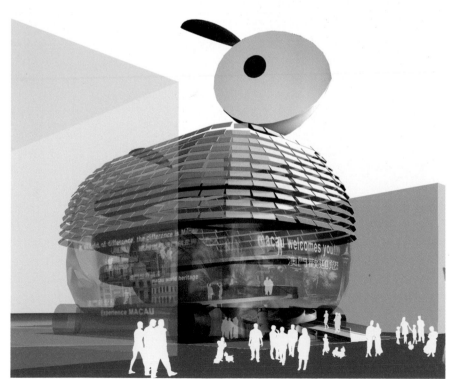

056

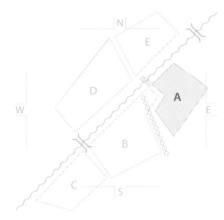

Morocco Pavilion

Theme

Art of Living in Morocco's Urban History

Zone	National Day	Year	Month	Day
A		2010	9	30

上海
世博会

Morocco is the only African country with a self-built pavilion, which aims to present the history of the cities and makes people better understand the Moroccan way of living. The neat outline and the wisdom and innovation embodied in the design make the pavilion an artwork. Exhibitions in the three-storey building present the country's rich cultural heritage, the art of life in modern cities, urban residents' expectations and local people's contemplation on history, culture, environment and urban development issues.

The pavilion is designed in a people-oriented manner as embodied in the use of building materials that offer the best possible comfort and the application of sophisticated audio, sound-proof, heat-proof and ecological technologies.

Exhibitions
Zone A

Nepal Pavilion

Theme

Tales of Kathmandu City:
Seeking the Soul of a City;
Explorations and Speculations

Zone	National Day	Year	Month	Day
A		2010	9	3

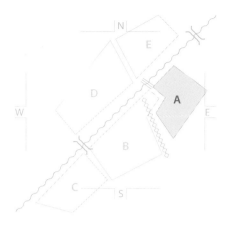

Nepal is world-renowned for its temples, pagodas, shrines and sanctuaries. The Nepal Pavilion is in the form of an ancient Buddhist temple, surrounded by traditional Nepalese houses, demonstrating the architectural and artistic genius of the Nepalese architects. The pavilion shows the development and expansion of cities via evolution of architectural forms. It focuses on the country's opportunities and challenges in environmental protection, and touches upon the soul of its cities by exploring their past and future. The pavilion highlights the glorious past of Kathmandu, the capital city of Nepal and an architectural, artistic and cultural center that has developed for over 1 000 years. Nepalese Buddhism is a mirror of its cultural environment and the cultural life of its people.

The pavilion is called Araniko Center, named after a great Nepalese architect—Araniko. The exhibits and decorative items are all handicrafts. The exquisite patterns on the wood carvings and potteries were made by 350 Nepalese households for almost two years. Superb carving technique and magnificent Buddhist architecture are of authentically Nepalese style. Nepal's artists, musicians, dancers and other performers give amazing shows.

Oman Pavilion

Oman — An Evolving Journey

Zone	National Day	Year	Month	Day
A		2010	7	22

Oman, one of the Arabian Gulf countries, boasts varied geographic features — sand beaches, mountain ranges, and deserts. Inspired by traditional sailing ships, the Oman Pavilion is shaped like an Arabian sailing boat. A stylized glass enclosure is reminiscent of the prow of traditional Omani sailing ships, a typical scene at Oman's old capital,

Nizwa and an Omani port city, Sohar. The pavilion is an organic body consisting of buildings, roads, green system and space environment, fully representing Oman's achievements in urban development and the image of the country.

The first exhibition section shows the varied geographic features of Oman. In the second section, visitors

are exposed to its cultural and social heritage. Oman's values of living in harmony with nature are the focus of the third section. It shows visitors the architecture, art and culture of its ancient cities, the city of desert, the city of mountains, the offshore city, the capital city Muscat and also the blue city to be completed in 2020. Oman's historic and cultural traditions

as well as its interpretations on city are displayed. The second section, drawing inspiration from the story *Sinbad: Legend of the Seven Seas*, launches a fantastic "tour" from Sohar to Muscat and to the 2020 blue city, and eventually back to Shanghai on a "magic carpet".

上海
世博会

Pakistan Pavilion

Theme

Harmony in Diversity in the City

Zone

A

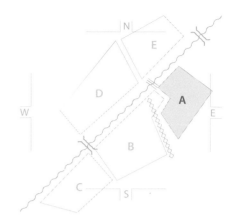

The Pakistan Pavilion is inspired by Lahore Fort. Creating a replica of the former imperial palace, the Islamic-style pavilion brilliantly interweaves traditions with modernity and culture with history. The combination of sound effects and multimedia technology serves to show the lifestyles of the urban and rural dwellers. The pavilion also probes into the challenges Pakistan is faced with in terms of education, science & technology, electricity supply and transportation in urban development.

Besides pictures and models, updated technologies such as holo-video are applied in showcasing Pakistan's brilliant past, which enables visitors to enjoy intelligent technologies and interactive experience. For example, visitors will learn about the culture and cities of Pakistan from electronic books, its ancient civilization and religion through water curtain projection, and its street vista in the theater. Pakistani clothes are exhibited, traditional dances are performed and a traditional restaurant serves authentically Pakistani delicacies including curry foods, BBQ, mango yogurt and milk tea.

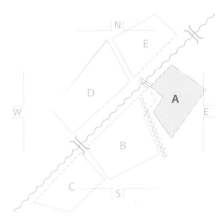

Qatar Pavilion

Theme

Ambitions of the Present and Aspirations of the Future

Zone	National Day	Year	Month	Day
A		2010	10	20

上海
世博会

Discovery of oil and natural gas has changed the lifestyle of the Qatari, and enabled Qatar's small villages to evolve into modern cities. In chronological order, the pavilion highlights the stellar achievements of Qatar to date, and offers a glimpse of its glorious future ahead, with a nod to the past. The pavilion, throughout which recurring Qatari motifs are interspersed, is reminiscent of Barzan Tower. The tower used to serve as an observatory platform to chart the calendar as well as a beacon welcoming returning pearl divers and fishermen and is lodged in the collective memory of all Qataris.

Also on display is an underwater seascape featuring two of Qatar's important undersea resources: pearls & oil. A fun quiz station, Bedouin tent, special handicraft and interactive videos illustrate how the country is intent on using green technology and modern initiatives to envisage sustainable cities. The Gallery within the pavilion will have regular exhibitions, including a collection in the Museum of Islamic Art, Egg Sculptures featuring Faberge eggs, Qatar's Stamp Exhibition and Children's Art Exhibition.

Republic of Korea Pavilion

Theme
Friendly City, Colorful Life

Zone	National Day	Year	Month	Day
A		2010	5	26

The exterior of the pavilion is decorated with Hangeul and art pixels. The open space without doors on the first floor delivers a message of "communication & integration". Four virtual guides, "B Girl", a foreign chef, a lady and an IT engineer, show visitors where to go.

My City section on the first floor offers a microscopic view of Seoul, containing the essence of the city such as a winding river, a water-surrounded stage, and streets teemed with creativity and vitality. The second floor — My life section focuses on culture, technology, humanity and nature. Another exhibition area My Dream envisages future technologies and provides information on the 2012 Yeosu Expo.

Saudi Arabia Pavilion

Theme

Unity within Diversity

Zone	National Day	Year	Month	Day
A		2010	9	23

上海
世博会

Saudi Arabia's urban development is growing rapidly like never before. Inspired by oasis, the pavilion, a "moon boat" elevated above the ground, features exotic Arabian gardens. Date palms are planted on the roof and the ground to provide shade. The pavilion, without doors and windows installed, promotes energy efficiency by utilizing the solar and wind power.

The exhibitions within the "boat" brief the visitors on Saudi Arabia's geography, population, history and politics, highlight four types of cities: a city of energy, a city of oasis, a city of ancient culture, and a city of new economy, as well as the country's experiences in urban development despite its climate and geography, and indicate that water, oil, knowledge are lifeline to Saudi Arabia's urban development. The pavilion includes a 3D theater with a 360° 1600 m² screen, almost the size of two football fields.

Sri Lanka Pavilion

Theme
Tradition to Modernity

Zone	National Day	Year	Month	Day
A		2010	7	18

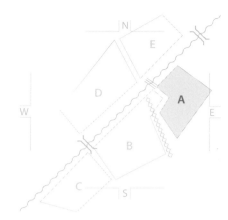

The exterior wall is decorated with plain national patterns to highlight the interior grandeur. The simple pavilion interprets the urban civilization from the historical perspective and reminds people to inherit traditions and brilliant cultures.

In the pavilion five unique cities are displayed via maps, models, pictures, etc. Anuradhapura is famous for economic prosperity, balanced ecology and sound religious environment; Sigiriya boasts charming primitive architecture based on reasonable use of resources; Polonnaruwa embodies that harmonious religions can promote social stability; Kandy features harmonious natural environment and traditional architecture; Galle exhibits the cultural integration of the Netherlands and Sri Lanka.

Taiwan Pavilion

Mountain, Water, Heart and Lantern — Nature, Soul and City

Zone
A

Taiwan Pavilion, bright and beautiful, is made up of a gable-roofed building, a huge glass sky lantern and LED sphere. The smart film covering the lantern's facade is transparent when wired up, through which visitors can see images on the LED; in case of power-off, images of local natural scenery can be projected on the facade.

The six display areas mainly use multimedia techniques. Among them, the Omnimax Theatre gives cyclic play of 4-minute movie of "Natural City", and the Window of Taiwan and City Living-Room also play movies; besides, the sky lanterns are released in an innovative way, thanks to the modern technology.

上海
世博会

Turkmenistan Pavilion

The distinctive grid shape integrated with simple modern architectural elements shows the charm of the country. The interior space features a combination of bright colors, brownish yellow and light gray. Real objects and multimedia present Turkmenistan's customs and geographical features and interpret the notions of Better City, Better Life and Oil Keeps the City Dream Alive.

The short video shows Turkmenistan's abundant tourist resources and tells the story of Akhal-Teke horses. Visitors can learn more about the country's nomadic culture from the infrared touch screen. High-tech means are adopted to display Turkmenistan's jewels, cultural relics and exquisite carpet-making techniques.

UAE Pavilion

Exploration of the theme "The Power of Dreams" in the historical, social and contemporary contexts focus on how economic prosperity, assisted by innovations in science and technology, enabled UAE to develop thriving urbanized communities where people of diverse cultures live and work in harmony. The pavilion draws inspiration from the undulating sand-dunes in the UAE's deserts. Thanks to the reflective nature of its outer covering, diffused light penetrates the building during the day and spectacularly illuminates it at night. With innovative environmental strategies, the pavilion creates a fascinating harmony between nature and architecture.

The pavilion includes five parts. Its theatre presents a widescreen movie entitled *In the Blink of an Eye* that makes a striking contrast between the moments when the UAE was just founded and today when standard of living and urban environment in the country are among the best in the world. Following two "young guides", visitors start a virtual journey — there is indeed no better way to gain a bird's-eye view of the many incredible places in the country.

上海
世博会

Uzbekistan Pavilion

Theme
The Crossroad of Civilizations

Zone	National Day	Year	Month	Day
A	Day	2010	8	31

EXPO 2010

Uzbekistan, an important place on the ancient Silk Road, houses a great wealth of historic monuments and artifacts. Today, a large number of ingeniously designed and highly diversified buildings find their way into the country's architectural scene. The exterior of Uzbekistan Pavilion is decorated with mirror wave-like acrylic plastic which refracts the sun rays. Outside the pavilion is a sculpture of stork — the bird of happiness and prosperity and the symbol of freedom and new life. The ornament at the entrance shows a brilliant blend of tradition and innovation.

The exhibitions consist of six sections: The Cities directing toward the Future, Ancient and Eternally Young Tashkent, The Cities of Progress and Creation, Harmony of City, Harmony of Rural Area, Life Style — Traditions and the Present, Uzbekistan Is the Country of Great Tourist Potential. The Cities of Progress and Creation demonstrates the development of the country's numerous cities. Uzbekistan Is the Country of Great Tourist Potential presents Uzbekistan as a treasure house of cultural heritages, including world-renowned ancient city — Khiva.

EXPO 2010 SHANGHAI CHINA OFFICIAL ALBUM

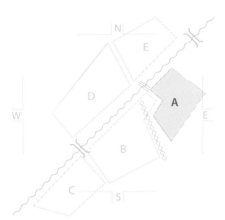

Vietnam Pavilion

The Millennium of Thang Long—Hanoi

Zone	National Day	Year	Month	Day
A		2010	9	2

上海
世博会

2010, a special year for Vietnam, marks the 1000th anniversary of the establishment of Hanoi as the capital. Hanoi, meaning "a city in rivers", is closely connected with nature. It is selected to reflect the harmony between city and nature. The wave-shaped exterior wall made of bamboos, the main material of the pavilion, resembles a river. And bamboos help to reduce the amount of heat from sunlight.

Inside the pavilion, bamboos are used to build a simple and unique palace to present celebrations for the 1000th anniversary of the establishment of Hanoi. After the Expo, all the bamboos will be re-used for welfare and school buildings.

070

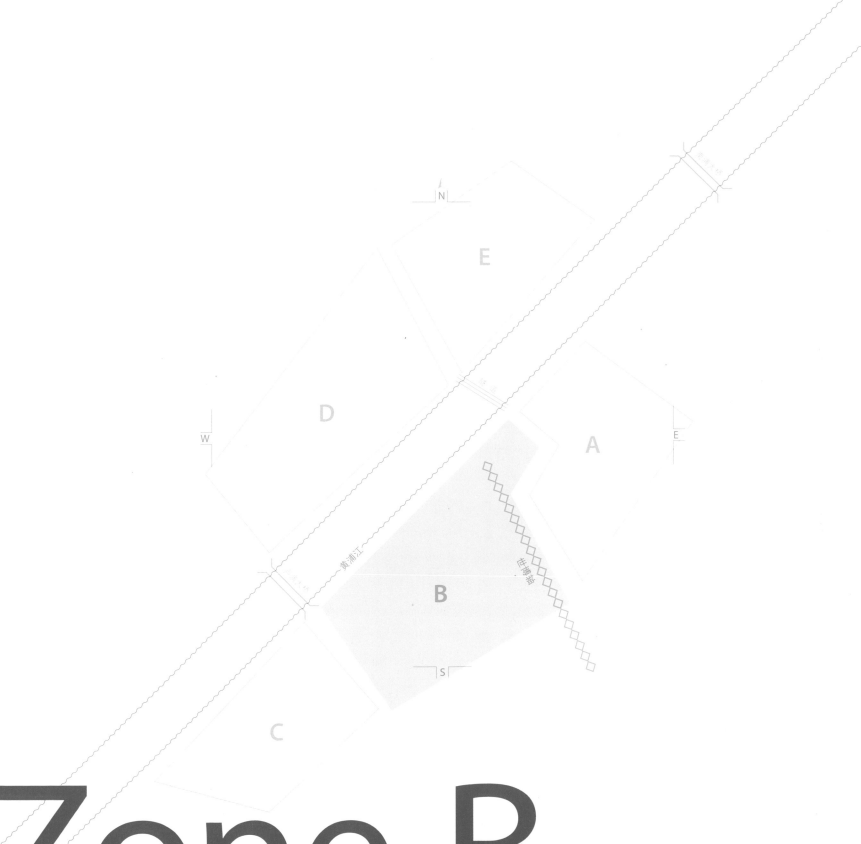

Zone B

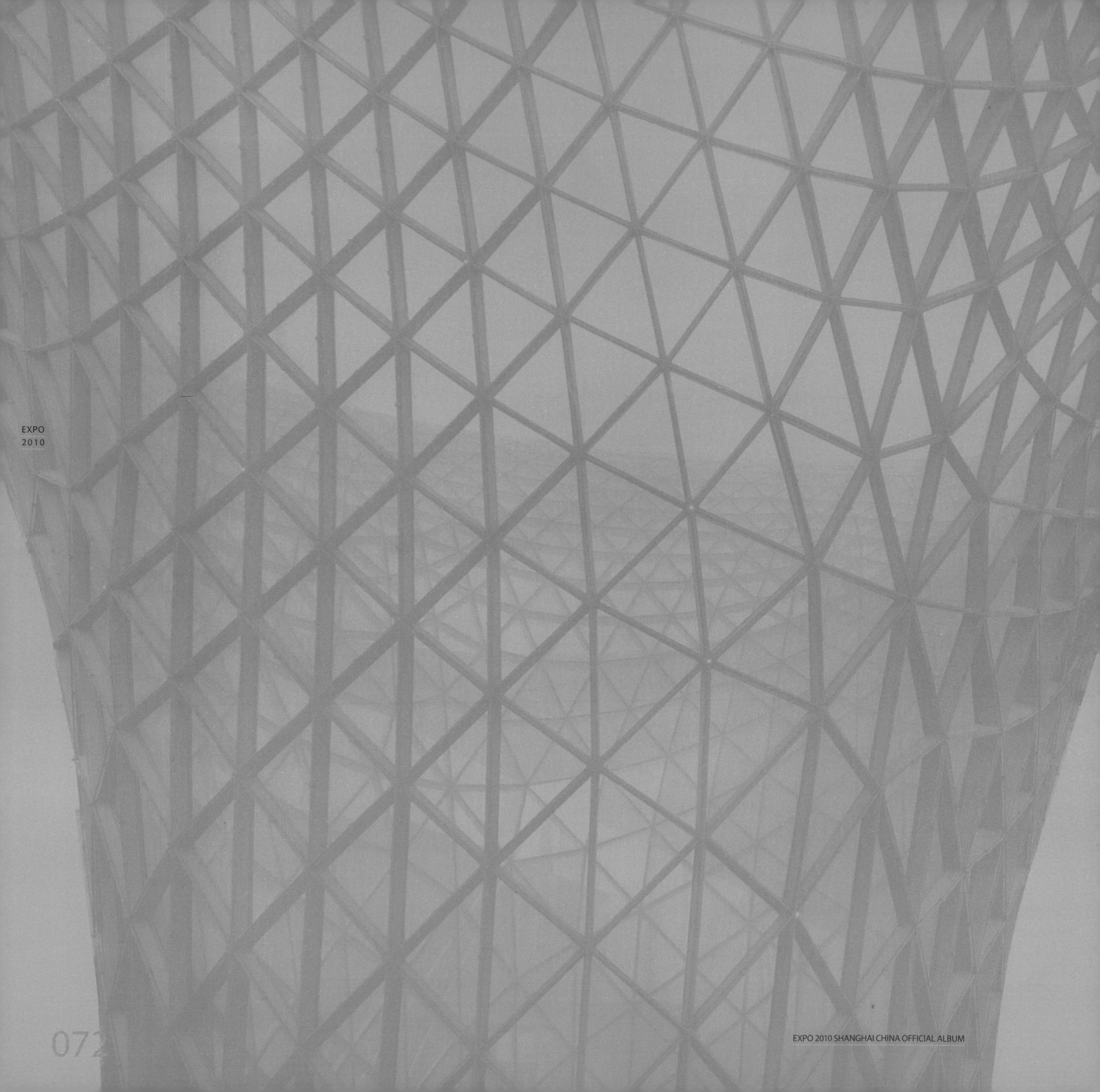

EXPO
2010

Australia Pavilion

Theme

ImagiNation

Zone	National Year Month Day
B	Day
	2010 6 8

上海
世博会

Besides koala and kangaroo, Australia boasts beautiful countryside views, vigorous modern cities and rich cultures. The curvy shape of the Australia Pavilion is evocative of the rocks in Australia's wilderness. The exterior wall of the pavilion is clad in special weather-proof steel that develops an increasingly deep, red ochre colour, evocative of the Australian outback.

The pavilion comprises three parts, illustrating Australia's indigenous species, cultural diversity and urban livability. Journey part assembles a totally-enclosed glass passage of 160 meters with six exhibition sections, displaying the history of Australia. Discover features a 1 000-seat theatre screening a multimedia show to explore the country's culture. Enjoy provides delicious food and wine and souvenirs unique to the country. Australian artists present fantastic programs to visitors.

Brunei Darussalam Pavilion

Theme
Now... for the Future

Zone	National Day	Year	Month	Day
B		2010	5	8

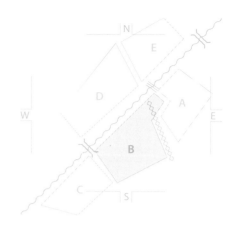

Blessed with oil and gas, Brunei has enjoyed a high standard of education and health care for 80 years. Now it has to meet people's immediate needs, and the long-term aspirations of future generations. It is the core design concept to introduce traditional lifestyle, preserve natural environment, maintain economic prosperity, improve the quality of people's lives, and honor the rich heritage and profound tradition. The circulative structure inside symbolizes Brunei's eight strategic plans and its preservation of nature.

The unique rainforest decorates the main entrance of the pavilion. The five sections show the country's objective of economic development and its history, tradition, culture and ancient sites through videos, posters, touch screens and 4D cinema. Hand-woven textiles and silver articles are sold in the pavilion.

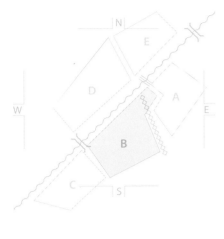

Cambodia Pavilion

Cambodian architecture in cities tells visitors about people's lifestyle when it was built and about the evolution of cities. The exhibition is about typical architecture of Angkor, Longvek and Phnom Penh periods which displays Cambodia's time-honored culture, art and rich natural resources and showcases its international awareness of protecting cultural heritage.

Ancient Cambodians built Angkor, capital of Khmer Empire, with stone. Angkor Period section presents visitors with stone buildings like palace, temple, road, bridge, reservoir and hospital. Longvek Period section displays the wide use of wood in urban construction. Phnom Penh Period section presents visitors with a capital city built of cement, gravel and sand and tells about the legend about the name "Phnom Penh".

DEVNET Pavilion

Theme

The City Rescue and Harmonious Life — Integrative International Communication & Cooperation

Zone	Honor Day	Year	Month	Day
B		2010	9	8

How to reduce natural disaster-inflicted loss and enable people to lead a harmonious life has become a global concern. That's also the thematic message DEVNET Pavilion tries to deliver. The pavilion has a crystal clear glass facade. Seven water-filled glass pillars are erected at the entrance to show the words of "Boundless Love" and other patterns constantly with the momentary fall difference of the water flowing in the pillars.

New findings in emergency rescue and energy-saving and environment-friendly products are displayed. Mascots including panda and dolls represent the hope for a better world. A charity walk of fame is set up to encourage love and support between people. The latest development of certain world famous brands, gold plates with 568 characters of Chinese surnames and precious Japanese exhibits are also on display.

International Red Cross and Red Crescent Pavilion

Theme
Humanity without Boundary

Zone	Honor Day	Year	Month	Day
B		2010	5	8

The theme "Humanity without Boundary" reflects the great value this organization has always placed on humanity, the organization's worldwide presence and its profound influence. The entrance of the pavilion is designed as a tent, which is most commonly used in disaster relief projects, creating a sense of "being there".

The pavilion is made up of three parts, showing a series of wars and other calamities, and presenting the organization's unremitting endeavors In relieving human suffering. Each visitor is presented with a red bracelet at the entrance. The theme wall captures the image of a visitor's face and red bracelet, and transmit it in real time to LCD on the wall. Visitors can see their pictures together with those of numerous volunteers.

Indonesia Pavilion

Theme
Indonesia Bio Diver City

Zone
B

EXPO
2010

Indonesia boasts beautiful natural landscape and diverse cultures, and its people live a simple but colorful life. As an important feature of the Indonesia Pavilion and a symbol of mixture of tradition and modern lifestyle, a number of bamboo sticks project out of the roof. A 600-meter passage runs through the building, at the center of which, a waterfall cascades down 17 meters. The exhibitions in the pavilion showcase Indonesia's picturesque scenes, marine life, culture and innovation.

The four-storey building is divided into different sections such as the Stage, Hall, and Multimedia Theater. Indonesian songs, dances and food are presented on the first floor, and a 3-meter-high sculpture of Zheng He and traditional Indonesian boats are shown on the second floor. Music bands are there to give performances, and interested visitors may join them to show their own musical talents.

Joint Pavilion of International Organizations

The joint pavilion incorporates the exhibitions of such organizations as Association of Southeast Asian Nations, Boao Forum for Asia, Common Market for Eastern and Southern Africa, Forum Francophone des Affaires, Global Environment Facility, International Association of Public Transport, International Council of Museums, International Network for Bamboo and Rattan, League of Arab States, Shanghai Cooperation Organization, World Organization of United Cities and Local Governments, World Water Council and World Wide Fund for Nature.

上海
世博会

Exhibitions
Zone B

Pavilion of Association of Southeast Asian Nations

Theme
ASEAN Community — One Vision, One Identity, One Community

Zone B

Established in 1967, ASEAN is now an organization promoting cooperation in politics, economy and security in Southeast Asia. The pavilion, whose design is inspired by the beautiful winding coastlines of the region, presents the shared vision of ASEAN states to create a harmonious life.

The pavilion provides general information on ASEAN and relevant agencies, and displays photos of the member states around the theme of "Better City, Better Life". Cultural and tourist information is displayed through posters, brochures, billboards, short movies and interactive media, reflecting the wishes for strengthened cooperation and a bright future.

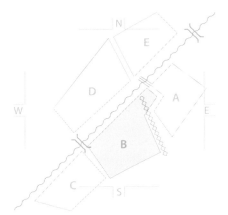

Pavilion of Boao Forum for Asia

Boao Forum for Asia — Asia, Searching for Win-Win

Zone
B

BFA wishes to bring Asian countries closer to their development goals by further integration of regional economy. The blue-and-silver hue adds a modern and international element to the pavilion.

The eye-catching main structure of the stand takes "ASIA" as its prototype. The spherical logo element together with a world map serves as the huge backdrop that symbolizes globalization, diversity and integration. Responding to the arc information desk, it also indicates "world in union" and sheds light to the significance of "understanding, communication, win-win cooperation and building harmonious cities for a better future". Tropical plants and modern exhibition stand showcase the coexistence of prosperous urban economy and environment, harmony and civilization.

上海
世博会

Pavilion of Common Market for Eastern and Southern Africa

The COMESA, formerly known as the Preferential Trade Area of Eastern and Southern Africa, is the largest and earliest regional economic organization established in Africa to realize economic integration by strengthening the trade and investment ties between its member states.

The pavilion, including areas for exhibition and interactive activities, presents the unique charms of COMESA states, and COMESA's efforts to establish a free trade area and promote balanced socioeconomic development in its member states. The giant mural vividly depicts the Eastern and Southern African people's daily life, and the short movies on the LED screen showcase the new faces of the member states.

Pavilion of Forum Francophone des Affaires

The City of Wonderful Life

Zone	Honor Day	Year	Month	Day
B		2010	6	18

Forum Francophone des Affaires, established in 1987 as a consortium of French-speaking enterprises, is the only non-governmental global economic organization recognized by French-speaking communities. The pavilion combines both traditional and modern elements. The "waterfall", on the exterior wall, waves between glass walls and the glazed tiles create a cool and refreshing atmosphere.

The pavilion is a high-tech glass-and-steel structure, illuminated by landscape lamps and decorated by murals from around the world, combining traditional arts and modern technologies. A stream of water runs through a cone hung from the wood-and-brass vault and flows into a glass shell, indicating the significant role of rainwater in world ecological balance.

上海
世博会

Pavilion of Global Environment Facility

Theme

Investing in Environmentally Friendly Technologies

Zone	Honor Day	Year	Month	Day
B		2010	7	20

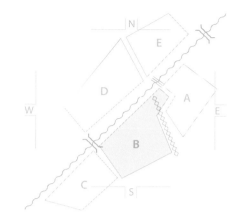

GEF provides grants or other financial supports for projects related to such areas as climate change, biodiversity, international waters and the ozone layer with a view to improving global environment and promoting sustainable development of the recipients. Mainly colored green, the pavilion is designed simple but delicate.

Pictures, multimedia and other means are taken to introduce the history, structure and development of the GEF, and the organization's contributions to experience sharing and the sound development of global environment.

Pavilion of International Association of Public Transport

Public Transport: Solutions for Our Future

Zone	Honor Day	Year	Month	Day
B		2010	8	28

The pavilion is designed to present global public transport development, summarize experiences, and explore the potential of public transport to change cities and urban life and create a better life. Integrating green elements, it introduces the merits of public transport in a visitor-friendly, intriguing and interesting way.

Visitors are impressed by the track and road models as well as videos and pictures that reflect achievements made in this field. The history of public transport over the past 125 years is reviewed together with many best practices of public transport and interesting examples of urban planning. Innovative public transport elements from around the world and winning entries in the UITP "Solutions for Our Future" Award essay contest are exhibited.

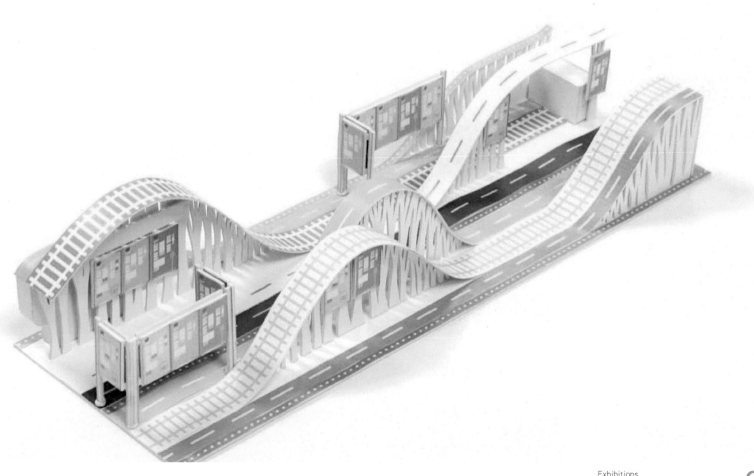

Pavilion of International Council of Museums

Theme
Museums, Heart of the City

Zone	Honor Day	Year	Month	Day
B		2010	5	18

The interdependence and interaction between museums and the city is explored in five aspects: culture, society, economy, innovation and environment. The simple yet modern pavilion introduces the international museum community and relevant industries to convey the council's purpose and duties.

The front circular space can serve as both a featured exhibit area and an activity area, and the video wall at the back creates a sensational experience of modern museum environment. The monthly-changing exhibitions each focus on one region to present diversified images of museums. There will be a series of activities and lectures centered on the theme.

Pavilion of International Network for Bamboo and Rattan

Bamboo and Rattan • Human Settlements • Environment

Zone	Honor Day	Year	Month	Day
B		2010	5	20

The INBAR is committed to promoting the sustainable use of bamboo and rattan and contributing to poverty eradication and environmental protection. The LED screen on the exterior presents short movies on the favorable living environment created by bamboo and rattan.

Bamboo and rattan is used to make the pavilion's exterior, interior and floor, which is, eco-friendly. Various exhibits made of bamboo and rattan, such as instruments, furniture, containers and ornaments, are displayed. The video column is a showcase for different bamboo structures in the world and the significance of bamboo and rattan to human life, advocating the idea of "replacing wood with bamboo".

上海
世博会

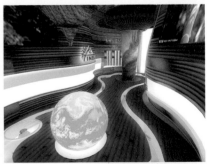

Pavilion of League of Arab States

Theme

Ancient & Modern Life of the Arab City:
One Language, One Civilization, 22 Cities

Zone **B**

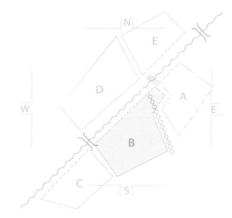

The League of Arab States is a regional organization dedicated to strengthening cooperative ties among Arab states. Incorporating 22 stands, the pavilion uses posters, books, PPT presentations, movies and internet access to introduce the activities of the LAS and call for world understanding and recognition.

The exhibition focuses on various aspects of life in ancient cities including culture, architecture, lifestyle, natural resources, trade and economy, and depict the urbanization progress of 22 ancient cities and the influence of historical changes on the Arabian life.

Pavilion of Shanghai Cooperation Organization

World Harmony Begins in the Neighborhood

Zone	Honor Day	Year	Month	Day
B		2010	6	15

The Declaration of Shanghai Cooperation Organization signed in Shanghai in 2001 marked the birth of the organization. Since then, cooperation has been carried out and increasingly strengthened in such fields as culture, trade and military affairs. The pavilion is a western-style structure inlaid with a Chinese antithetical couplet featuring the exhibition theme. Its dynamic exterior design inspires imaginations of people cheerfully dancing and stepping forward to Shanghai hand by hand.

Inside, the walls and the dome unfold a magnificent scene of sunrise and rosy glow, symbolizing a bright and promising future of SCO. The 11.1m-long golden relief on the floor records the milestones in SCO's history and exhibits territories of its member states.

上海
世博会

Pavilion of United Cities and Local Governments

Theme
Men and Women for Better Cities

Zone
B

Cities indicate the development of human civilization and are the platforms of modern economic, technological, information and social activities. Local governments administrate cities and regions and play important roles in economic and social development and offering better life for local people. UCLG was founded in May 2004, with its secretariat in BarcelonaIt consists of governmental associations of 112 countries/regions and over 1000 cities of 95 countries/regions.

The roofless pavilion aims to promote cooperation, mutual respect and unity between members of various development phases and cultures. It has a Reception Area, an Exhibition Area, a Recreational Area and a Members Area. In the Exhibition Area 8 touch screens offer information on UCLG's 8 sections. With a touch on the screen, visitors can see his/her home country/region highlighted on the globe. In the Recreational Area visitors may interact through the screen with people online. The Members Area has communication/cooperation places.

Pavilion of World Water Council

Theme
Water for Life and Development

Zone	Nonor Day	Year	Month	Day
B		2010	6	26

Of the global water resources, only 3% is fresh water, of which less than 1% can be used by human being. The World Water Council endeavors to raise public awareness of water issues on the basis of sustainable development of the environment, so as to improve the preservation, exploitation and management of water resources.

The pavilion focuses on the role of water in creating better cities for a better life and showcases successful and innovative ways of managing water for cities and citizens. Highlighting a variety of subjects, the exhibition focuses on challenges that various regions are facing with, such as natural disasters, the Millennium Development Goals, financing for water and climate change. Children are invited to learn about water through hands-on activities in the Kid's Corner which provides information on water challenges and solutions.

上海
世博会

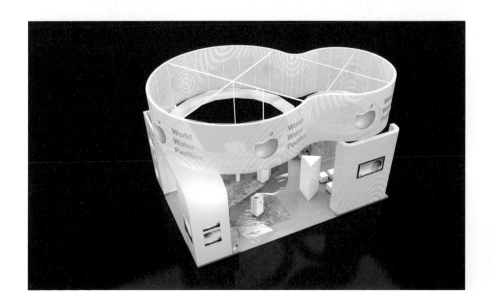

Pavilion of World Wide Fund for Nature

Theme
River, Estuary and City

Zone	Honor Day	Year	Month	Day
B		2010	6	5

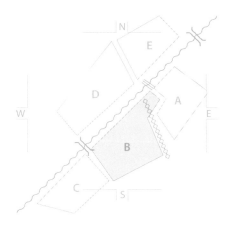

The WWF, established in 1961 as an independent NGO, has gained reputation for its commitment to environment protection. Adopting Tai Chi elements, the pavilion is designed to showcase the organization's global achievements in the past 50 years, and particularly its philosophy of sustainable development of rivers, estuaries and cities against climate change.

Modern interactive devices are employed to explain the causes and impacts of climate change. Entering the "estuary", visitors will know about the development of and environment protection in such cities as Rotterdam, London, New York and Shanghai. The exterior and interior walls are both decorated with giant children's drawings interpreting the exhibition theme and depicting the future urban life in children's eyes.

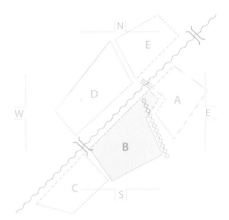

Life Sunshine Pavilion

Eliminate Discrimination and Poverty, Cherish Life and Share Sunshine; City Offers Better Life for the Disabled

Zone	Theme Week	Year	Month	Day
B		2010	5	10~16

上海
世博会

The first-ever Expo pavilion set up to show the life and talents of the disabled, the pavilion, via introducing the Chinese and global cause for the disabled, makes the public know and care more about the disabled while look into their beautiful future.

The pavilion is divided into a Pre-show, Life section, Sunshine section and Corridor of Love. In the Life section, the movie *Life Miracle* is screened, calligraphic works, paintings and photos of the disabled are exhibited, and experience of their daily life is presented. In the Sunshine section, visitors can learn more about the disabled and the hi-tech assistant equipment specially made for them. In particular, the 6th version of *My Dream* makes its debut in the pavilion.

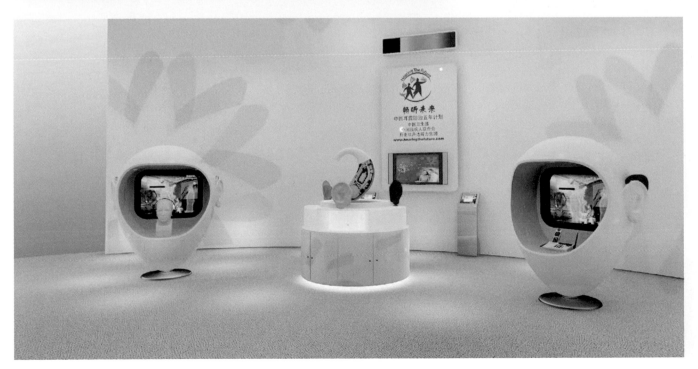

Malaysia Pavilion

Theme

One Malaysia — City Harmonious Living

Zone	National Day	Year	Month	Day
B	Day	2010	9	12

Malaysia lays stress on unity between its different ethnic groups and promotion of local cultures. The pavilion is composed of two gracefully sloping roofs supported by colonnades, and resembles a sailing boat when viewed afar. Its rooftop structure is typical traditional Malaysian architecture and the sightseeing elevator draws inspiration from the Twin Towers in Kuala Lumpur. Its exterior wall design is inspired by traditional fabric painting and dyeing in the country and consists of butterflies, flowers, birds and geometrical patterns.

Visitors may appreciate the charm of the world cultural heritage sites such as Penang and Malacca, play mini golf and traditional indoor games, experience truly Malaysian urban life and watch the making of exquisite works of art.

MeteoWorld Pavilion

For Safety and Well-being of the People

The pavilion is composed of four cloud-shaped oval globes. While presenting various meteorological wonders, it calls for people to make efforts in saving energy and reducing emissions. The exterior wall takes a bright white membrane structure with evenly-distributed sprayers. When they are on to produce a misty effect, a beautiful rainbow can be seen in the sun.

Within the pavilion, visitors can take a "hot-air balloon" ride, cross the "climate corridor", experience weather changes in the 4D Cinema and weather forecast in Expo Observatory, and learn more about the services of a future observatory and the role of a disaster early-warning system in a city's disaster prevention and mitigation.

World Meteorological Organization (Honor Day: May 9), European Organization for the Exploitation of Meteorological Satellites and Group on Earth Observations collaborate in the pavilion design and exhibition.

上海世博会

New Zealand Pavilion

Cities of Nature: Living between Land and Sky

Zonez	National Day	Year	Month	Day
B		2010	7	9

New Zealanders believe that combination of natural landscape and environmental protection ensures a quality life in modern cities. The wing-shaped pavilion evokes the image of the land of long white clouds. The remarkable design of the pavilion, especially its rooftop garden, highlights the natural beauty of the country and technological innovation of its people. Its structure encompasses cultural, scenic and humane elements such as white clouds, gardens and natural scenes.

In the welcoming space, visitors can enjoy Maori dance performed by the indigenous people and have a close look at the Maori columns. A 112-meter-long multimedia corridor exhibits hundreds of pictures, displaying New Zealand's customs, geography & scenery. The special effects team of *The Lord of the Rings* brings to life a panoramic image of the country. Also on display is a 1.8-ton jade boulder that is to amaze many of the visitors.

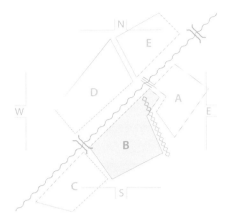

Pacific Joint Pavilion

Theme

Pacific — An Inspiration to Cities!

Zone

B

The Pacific Joint Pavilion encompasses the exhibitions of 14 Pacific countries including Cook Islands (National Day: August 5), Fiji (National Day: August 6), Kiribati (National Day: July 12), Marshall Islands (National Day: August 17), Micronesia (National Day: August 29), Nauru (National Day: October 26), Niue (National Day: October 19), Palau (National Day: October 23), Papua New Guinea (National Day: September 17), Samoa (National Day: August 1), Solomon Islands (National Day: July 27), Tonga (National Day: August 2), Tuvalu (National Day: October 13), Vanuatu (National Day: October 8), and two international organizations including SPTO (Honor Day: May 12) and PIF (Honor Day: May 12).

The pavilion, with a plain appearance, is decorated in a unique style inside. Sixteen woven single sails, symbolizing the 16 participants, show their marvelous natural landscape, distinct cultural environment and local customs.

上海
世博会

Pavilion of Public Participation

Theme
Our Home

Zone
B

As the only pavilion featuring public participation in the Expo Site, it highlights the idea "each action you take will change your life". Focusing on the theme "Our Home", it adopts modern interactive facilities (Internet, radio and television network, computer, cell phone, etc) for visitors to participate in the exhibition. Randomly changed exhibits show its openness and flexibility. A piece of "paper" in constant change records and witnesses the history of mankind-driven urban development.

Tens of thousands of photos display the history of world exposition, and a 4m×16m scroll adds to the magnificence. Visitors can upload their photos, communicate face-to-face with celebrities and design their ideal city in the pavilion.

Pavilion of World Trade Centers Association

Theme
Peace and Stability Through Trade

Zone	Honor Day	Year	Month	Day
B		2010	6	9

The pavilion exterior can gradually change its color from sky blue to grass green, implying a harmonious world and WTCA's vision for peace and stability through trade.

The first section Kaleidoscope of World Trade displays videos about different cities around the world. The second section Around the World through World Trade Centers enable visitors to understand WTCA's development and its history. The third section is known as World Trade, shedding light on different cities' trade development initiatives. Seminars and conferences are held and broadcasted on the WTCA official website and online participation of people around the world is encouraged.

上海
世博会

Exhibitions
Zone B

Philippines Pavilion

Theme
Performing Cities

Zone	National Day	Year	Month	Day
B		2010	6	9

The pavilion conveys a message to the world that music and dance make people creative and the city dynamic. Its exterior is covered with transparent diamond-shaped objects that can create special visual effect. The four elevations are decorated with catchy collages of various hands, calling attention to humanity and the relationship between people. The exhibition features stage performances where music is integrated with celebrations to show the happy life people are enjoying.

Entering the pavilion, visitors can see a large stage which has a sail-like decoration and can change its scene as the exhibition theme changes.

Spectacular performances showcase the collision and fusion between various cultures in the country and how positive, independent and carefree its people are. The best Philippine cuisine and coffee is available in the café of the boutique section. In the enclosed spa experience area, visitors can enjoy traditional Philippine spa massage.

Singapore Pavilion

Theme

Urban Symphony

Zone	National Day	Year	Month	Day
B		2010	8	7

The pavilion looks like a huge "music box", whose sound pleases the ears of visitors. It is made of recyclable materials. The exterior design with slots and the cold pool around central area on the first floor help adjust the temperature inside the pavilion. At night, brilliant light shines out through the scattered windows and slots on the exterior wall, lending charm to the "music box". Its exhibition sections of different shapes are linked up by gentle slopes and stairs. Music fountain, audiovisual interplay and distinctive flowers on the roof garden compose a harmonious symphony and a miniature Singapore.

The second floor is a pillarless exhibition hall of nearly 600 square meters. It includes three circular theaters, showing videos of performances by Singaporean popular stars and reflecting Singapore's originality and diverse cultures. A tropical garden on the top floor inspires people's imagination about a garden city.

上海
世博会

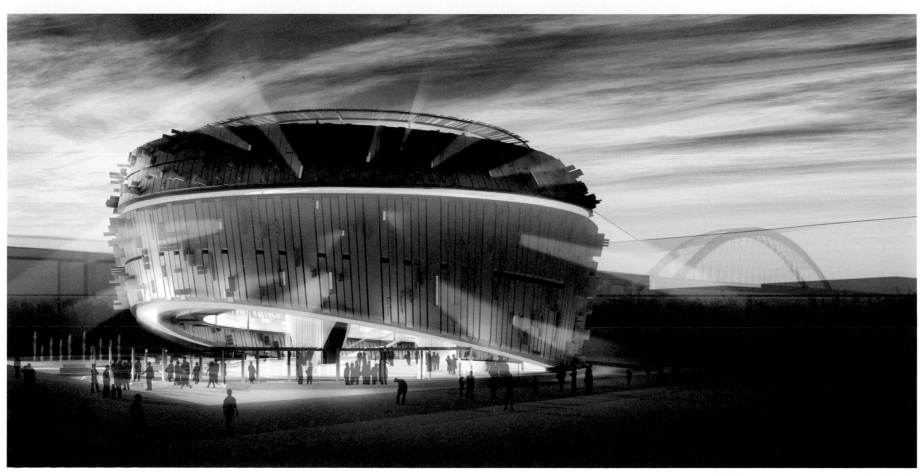

Thailand Pavilion

Theme

Thainess: Sustainable Ways of Life

Zone	National Day	Year	Month	Day
B		2010	9	5

The pavilion, made up of elegant structures, emphasizes the concept of "Thainess". A palette of red and gold adorns the pavilion. Elements of Thai's traditional art and architecture and Thai lifestyle are incorporated. Sophisticated audiovisual technologies are employed to show Thai's history & culture and its changes that come with the globalizing currents, and show people's pursuit of world peace.

A Journey of Harmony introduces the lifestyle in early Thailand and the integration between ethnic groups and cultures. Harmony over Diversity depicts the interaction between its urban and rural communities, and its long-standing friendly relations with other countries. Happiness through Harmony illustrates how the Thais value a life of simplicity that follows the idea of "sufficiency" in all things they do.

102

UN Joint Pavilion

Theme
One Earth, One UN

Zone **B**

The UN Joint Pavilion displays the successful practices of the UN system in such fields as sustainable development, fighting the climate change and urban management.

Participating organizations of the pavilion include FAO, IAEA, IMO, ITU (Honor Day: May 17), UNAIDS, CBD, UNFCCC, UN-HABITAT, UN (Honor Day: October 24), UNCDF, UNICEF, UNCTAD, UNESCO, UNEP, UNHCR, UNIDO, UNFPA, WB, WHO, WIPO, UNWTO and WTO.

上海
世博会

104

Zone C

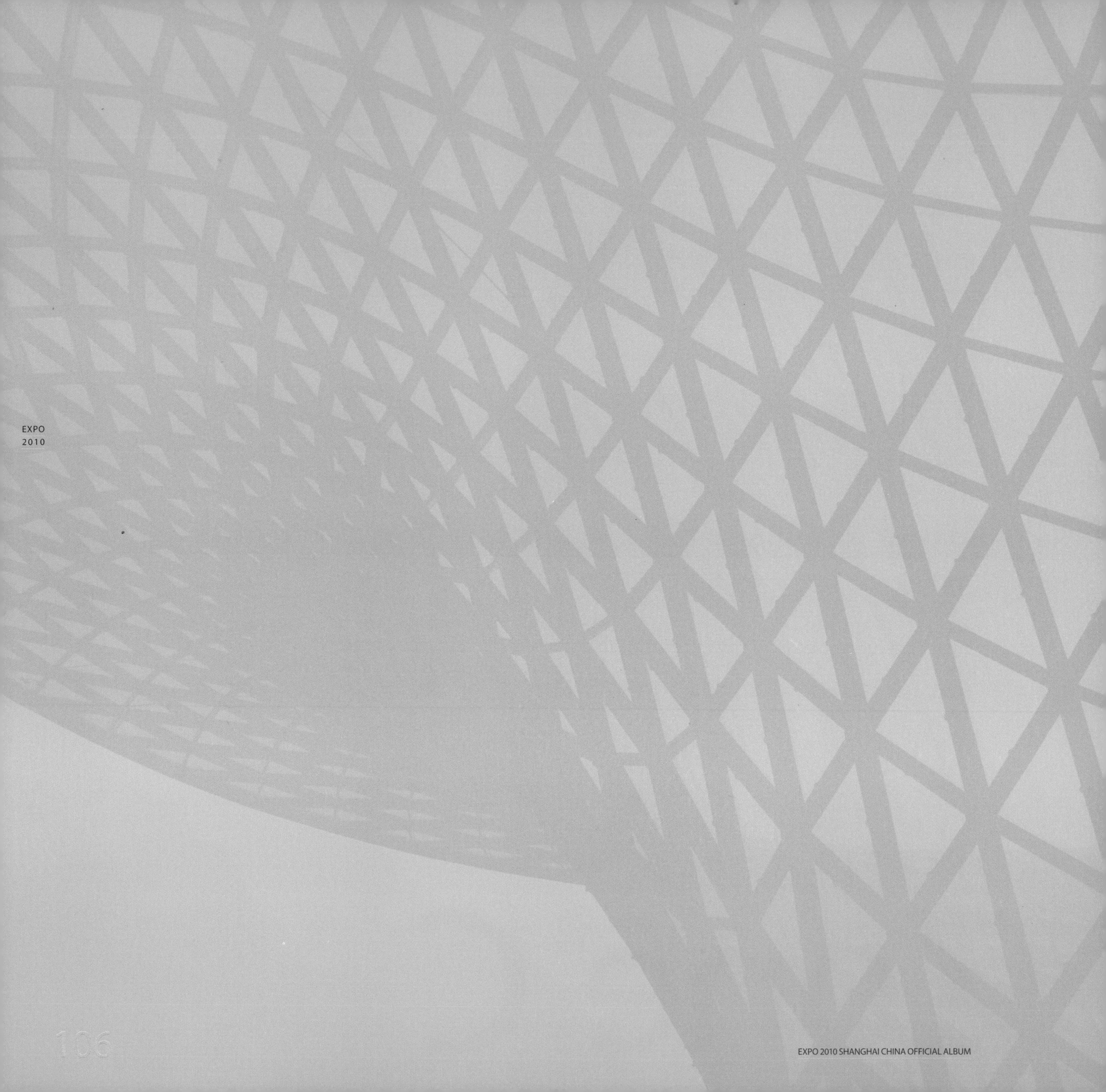

Africa Pavilion

Africa Pavilion is the largest one among the joint pavilions at Expo 2010. It is composed of 43 independent pavilions. Forty-two countries along with the African Union organize exhibitions in the pavilion, which harbors the largest number of participants from Africa in the history of the world expositions.

Distinctive African elements and features are embodied in the patterns on the facades. The luxuriant and towering tree is a symbol of the extraordinary vitality of the continent. The strong root stretches deep into the earth, implying that Africa is the origin of civilization. The tree absorbs nutrition from the earth through its root, so that it can reach for the sky. Likewise, Africa is a land of hope and opportunity by drawing strength from indigenous African cultures.

There is also a public area for performances, which consists of a performance stage, a reality show platform, and an exhibition area.

African Union (AU) Pavilion

Theme

Clean Energy for Better Management of Mega African Cities

Zone	Honor Day	Year	Month	Day
C	Day	2010	6	3

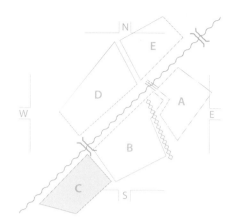

Covering subjects such as transportation, buildings, schools, hospitals, national parks and public facilities, the pavilion illustrates the key role clean energy plays in urban development and improving life.

At the entrance, a gigantic African primitive sculpture with words on it echoes the glimmering globe afar, indicating how important Africa is in environmental protection and coordination of world affairs. In the central round area, visitors can watch movies about urban development in Africa, particularly about environmental protection and the use of clean energy. Along the curving corridor, visitors can learn about development of African countries, urban transformation, economic rise and cultural heritage in Africa.

Benin Pavilion

Theme

Insertion of Village Territory in Cities as Engine for Sustainable Development

Zone	National Day	Year	Month	Day
C		2010	10	6

Benin is a developing country with growing cities and rural areas in transition.

The exterior design of the pavilion draws inspiration from the Royal Palace of Abomey and traditional residential buildings "TATA" which look like chateaux. The external appearance of the building is bright and warm with rich colors. The central element in the design of Benin Pavilion is the "Fishing Boat", which, together with local handicrafts and artistic decoration, helps to showcase the urbanization process in Benin and indicates that urbanization is the driving force for the sustainable development of cities.

The pavilion is divided into two exhibition areas: the central area and the secondary area. The central area mainly displays the cultural attractions, traditional housing, arts and handicrafts. Here, visitors can know about the rich history and culture of the country. In addition, through the exhibition of highly valuable handicrafts such as bronze reliefs, wood carvings, copper sculptures and ivory carvings, the fascinating and colorful life in Benin is presented to visitors. The secondary area showcases the countryside and cities of Benin as well as the country's contemplation on interaction between rural and urban areas.

Botswana Pavilion

Theme
A Heritage of Peace

Zone	National Day	Year	Month	Day
C		2010	7	21

The fusion of urban and rural cultures and a better life enjoyed by all are what "A Heritage of Peace" is meant for. The pavilion, simple and unadorned, takes brown as its dominant hue and adopts such architectural elements as dome, column and curved wall. The exhibitions within the pavilion tell about the urbanization of Botswana, a country of tourist attractions, commercial opportunities and favorable environment.

There are three exhibition areas. The Beautiful Botswana area mainly presents fascinating natural attractions and abundant mineral resources. The History and Heritage area focuses on the heritages, culture and art, people's daily life and the modernization process of Botswana, highlighting the significance of technology to the nation and its people. The City and Life area tells about the influence of resources and culture on urban development and the importance of a stable, secure and sustainable environment.

Burundi Pavilion

Theme

Coexistence of Man and Nature

Zone	National Day	Year	Month	Day
C		2010	7	3

Burundi is located to the south of the equator in the central-eastern Africa. With diversified landforms (mainly lakes and highlands) and natural conditions, the country attaches great importance to human-nature interaction. The exhibition in the pavilion emphasizes Burundi's achievements in sustainable development and economic resurrection, as well as the win-win relationship between cities and villages.

The pavilion consists of four areas. The Welcome area offers general information on Burundi. The Display area exhibits agricultural and fishery products and handicrafts, reflecting the interdependence between man and nature. In the Performance area, world famous Burundian drummers and dancers in traditional costumes present visitors something authentically Burundian. The Pub & Restaurant area serves Burundian coffee, tea and pastries from the Lake Tanganyika area.

上海
世博会

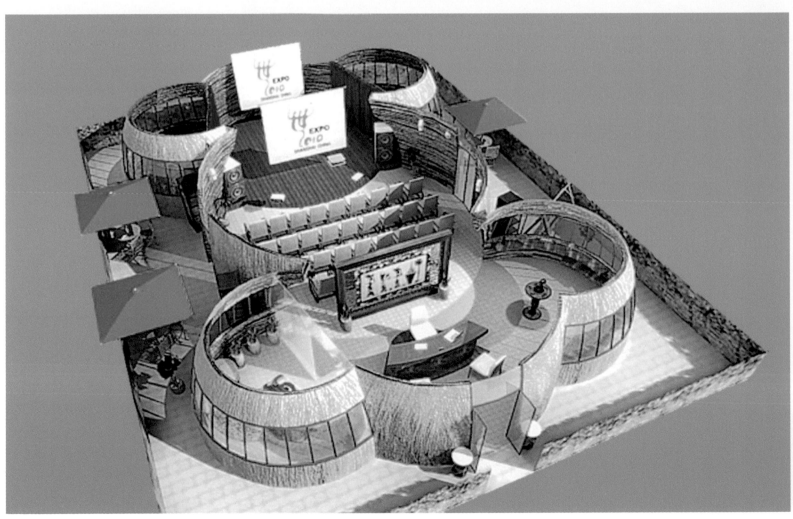

Cameroon Pavilion

Theme

Remodeling of Communities in the City

Zone	National	Year	Month	Day
C	Day	2010	10	3

Cameroon is injecting novelty into its traditional lifestyle. With a big tree as its centerpiece, the pavilion simulates various natural settings like plateaus, beaches and rain forests. Green, yellow and blue colors are cleverly used to embody the harmony between nature and mankind, the new look of old cities as well as the modern and romantic elements added to traditional communities.

The dense canopy of the tree covers almost the entire pavilion, symbolizing communities, traditional culture, vitality and effective protection of forests. The dwelling houses around the tree are of cultural value and reflect the transformation of communities and the people's aspirations. Visitors are presented with local tropical fruits, unique handiworks and fascinating performances, and can even show their skills on the simulated football field.

Cape Verde Pavilion

Located in the mid-Atlantic, the archipelago of Cape Verde is formed by volcanoes. The pavilion's entrance simulates Cape Verde's island topography. The exhibition shows the country's history & culture, modern cities and future economic development, showcasing the wisdom of a small island country to develop in the waves of globalization.

A subsiding sand table in the center displays the country's geo-landscape and the area around the table showcases its dynamism of using port cities to develop economy. In simulated sound of waves and sea breeze, visitors get to know the history of the island and feel its passion. Multimedia is used to display the charm of Creole Heritage and islanders' wisdom in conquering harsh conditions.

上海
世博会

Central African Republic Pavilion

Theme
Prosperity of Urban Economy

Zone	National Day	Year	Month	Day
C		2010	9	25

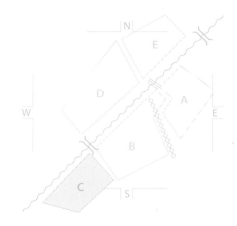

Urban culture is usually shaped by geographical conditions, historical changes, immigration, etc. during its formation and development. Interaction between diverse cultures also facilitates urban development and the prosperity of urban economy as well as the realization of the goal for a better life. Coupling simplicity of nature with flamboyance of modern elements, the pavilion showcases urban prosperity as well as the better life it brings to urban residents.

At the entrance area of the pavilion, visitors can walk along a meandering path and watch the rare creatures of the country. With the passionate Pygmy music, they will experience the genuine ecology of Central African Republic. In the area displaying resources and economy, visitors can see the country's typical dwellings with dome, cotton bedding, coffee beans, precious wood furniture exquisite, handicrafts, as well as curtains and decorations inlaid with diamond. At a stage area, people from Central African Republic heighten the ambiance with energetic folk dances for the visitors. In the area of future, the walls are posted with pictures of children's smiling faces, each reflecting a hope for the future.

EXPO 2010

Chad Pavilion

Chad, located in the inland of Central Africa, is far from the sea and one third of its territory is desert. It is thus fully aware of the significance of urban planning. Featured by Yardang landform, the pavilion employs pictures, movies, interactive multimedia and exhibits to express the idea of improving living conditions through harmonious development of mankind, cities and nature based on farsighted urban planning.

The Entrance area screens movies about the magnificent sceneries and the warm-hearted people, the Urban Planning area shows traditional dome houses and city planning, and the Economy and Resource area expresses the concept of oil-based economic growth and urban development. In the Interactive Area, visitors can learn about Chadian folkways. Besides, they can find enthralling fabrics, jewelries and other specialties displayed or offered for sale.

上海
世博会

Comoros Pavilion

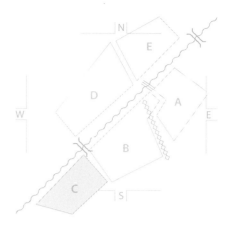

EXPO
2010

Comoros, born as a result of volcano eruption, is an island country in the Indian Ocean. Endowed with diversified landforms and rich biological resources, it is highlighted in the global efforts for conservation. Reflecting Comoros' topographical features, the pavilion includes City, Volcano and Ocean areas. Visitors will get familiar with its unique species, landscapes and civilization, and its practice and exploration of city and ecotourism coexistence.

In the miniature "Old Vendredi Mosque", visitors will see Arabian-style structures, spectacular wedding ceremonies and a coelacanth model. The "Kartala Volcano", on the verge of eruption, tells about the origin of Comoros civilization and presents its wildlife and unique topography. In the central area of the pavilion and surrounded by the "sea" and "coast" painted on the floor are three booths, each assuming the shape of and displaying information on Grande Comore, Moheli and Anjouan Islands separately.

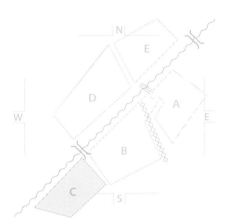

Republic of the Congo Pavilion

Theme

Natural Life in the Modern Setting (Bio-Diversity, Culture, Development and Tourism)

Zone	National Day	Year	Month	Day
C		2010	6	16

上海
世博会

Republic of the Congo, located in central-west Africa, is an agriculture-based multi-ethnic country. The pavilion is designed as a city neighboring the countryside to present the country's rich natural resources, unique biodiversity, valuable historic heritages and the achievements of modern development, signifying the good wish for harmonious urban-rural interaction and coexistence of man and nature.

Exhibition areas for History & Culture, Economy & Natural Resources, and Art & Interaction are connected by a tale of a fish Duoduo saving his friend Lele. In History & Culture area, the train indicates the country's running into the future, a symbol of farewell to the past and moving towards the world. In the Economy & Natural Resources area, the cargo ship indicates an open economy and the videos in the ship showcase Congo's achievement in modernization. In the Art & Interaction area which is a simulated beach, the ship-and-port exhibition wall shows the country's confidence to embrace the world.

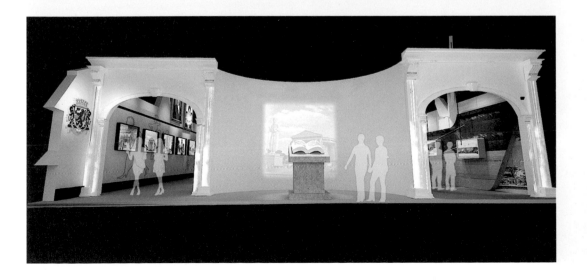

Côte d'Ivoire Pavilion

Theme

Cohabitation of Diverse Cultures in the City

Zone	National Day	Year	Month	Day
C		2010	8	8

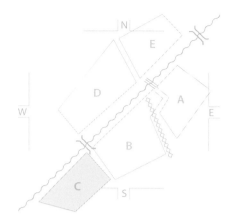

Côte d'Ivoire, a multi-ethnic country on the west coast of Africa, is rich in natural resources, particularly forest resources. The pavilion, mainly colored black, has a vinyl paint fence and mountain-shaped wall around it. Inside the pavilion, the exhibition area is designed based on tribal dwellings, presenting a modern and traditional Côte d'Ivoire, which shares its thoughts on maintaining harmony of diversified cultures and keeping the unique identity of different ethnic groups.

Exhibition area of Tradition displays cases on conserving and carrying on historical heritage and stories about cultural fusion and collision with photos. Economy area presents the country's predominating agricultural economy and today's urban economy influenced by modern culture. In exhibition area of Environment, on one side are cities in modernization; on the other, there are beautiful seas, plains and primitive forests, highlighting the harmonious coexistence of man and nature.

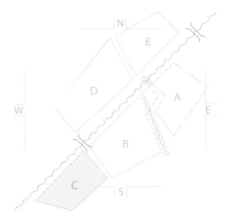

Democratic Republic of the Congo Pavilion

Theme

More Harmonious and Prosperous City, More Treasures

Zone	National Day	Year	Month	Day
C		2010	6	23

Democratic Republic of the Congo presents in a natural and pure style its unique features and the importance of proper use of rich resources in urban development and prosperity. The pavilion design presents the charm of the country in a natural and pristine environment.

Exhibition in the main area, where an abstract and bright-colored mine is presented, focuses on the theme of Impression and Reproduction. The mine represents the country's rich mineral resources. Impression starts from resources and displays the country's geo-landscape and historical background through texts, images and models. Reproduction centered around human beings displays real living environment and customs through real objects and reproduced scenes. The secondary exhibition area, focusing on the theme of Development, displays some symbolic monuments and statues to show the course of urban development and invite visitors to envision the bright future of this country.

Djibouti Pavilion

Theme

Djibouti, Economic Hub

Zone	National Day	Year	Month	Day
C		2010	6	30

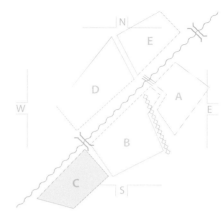

Djibouti displays its culture, rich tourist resources, and its glamour as a large international harbor based on its own geographical, cultural and economic background. One end of the pavilion is the traditional dwelling of nomadic Afar people "daboita" decorated amidst water and linked by a bridge to the other end which consists of Business and Leisure areas.

The "daboita" as the main exhibition area is covered with hand-woven belts on the top; the exterior side walls and the floor are laid with hand-woven tapestries and carpets. Djibouti paintings and handmade ornaments are hung on the interior wall, displaying the country's culture and prospect of development. Documentaries on the Republic of Djibouti are played in loop on a plasma screen. People in Djibouti can see the "daboita" through the Internet, sharing the joy of visitors to the Expo.

Equatorial Guinea Pavilion

Theme

Sustainable Beauty of the City

Zone	National Day	Year	Month	Day
C		2010	8	15

上海
世博会

Equatorial Guinea, located in Central Africa, has abundant forestry, fishing and oil resources. The pavilion is divided into three exhibition areas Seaside Scenery, Energy Exploitation and Utilization and Urban Future, displaying the shared past, present and future of nature and city and how the country reaches a balance between environment and development in the process of urbanization.

Entering the pavilion on the waves of the sea, visitors can walk through the Bioko Island, the Benito River, and up to the Pico Basilé Mountain, where the statue of Saint Mary stands. Beautiful Spanish-style architectures are among coconut groves and cocoa trees. Energy Exploitation and Utilization displays the country's rapid economic growth driven by oil exploitation and infrastructure construction. Urban Future exhibits the country's bright future in industry, agriculture, tourism and education.

Eritrea Pavilion

Theme
The Philosophy and Development of Urbanization in Eritrea

Zone	National Day	Year	Month	Day
C		2010	5	25

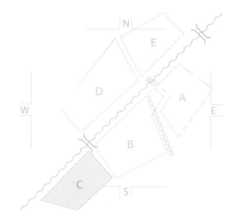

In the pavilion, the harmonious urban development of Eritrea is showcased in the following four aspects: Social Harmony, Social Justice, Environmental Protection, as well as Conservation and Use of Historical Heritage.

The pavilion is to showcase the progress that Asmara (which means "city of balance")and its satellite urban areas have made in infrastructure and social services. Visitors can also know more about the city of cohesion and social responsibility by the exhibition on its rich cultural heritage and different lifestyles. Eritrea's beautiful landscape, diversified marine life, measures on environmental improvement, archaeological discoveries, restoration of old railways, as well as relaxing, harmonious rural life are also presented to visitors by means of posters, slideshows, short movies, historical remains, artworks and architecture models.

Blended Legacy of Cities: the Ethiopian Experience

Zone	National Day	Year	Month	Day
C		2010	9	10

Ethiopia is located in the East Africa. Its pavilion shows Ethiopia's centuries of civilization, wisdom and urbanization progress, as well as its inclusive manner in protecting traditions and vestiges and addressing urban challenges.

There are three exhibition areas: the Ancient City—Harar Jugol, the Story of Coffee and the Eight World Heritage Sites. In the Ancient City—Harar Jugol, visitors can take a walk through the city gate and walls and along the streets, and find old buildings including the oldest mosque in Africa and the former residence of the French poet Rimbaud. The life scenes in the ancient city will unfold before visitors. Visitors can have a rest or join in coffee parties under a huge umbrella with local features, and will be attracted by the exhibition on eight world heritage sites.

上海
世博会

Gabon Pavilion

Theme

Interaction between Urban and Rural Areas

Zone	National Day	Year	Month	Day
C		2010	7	30

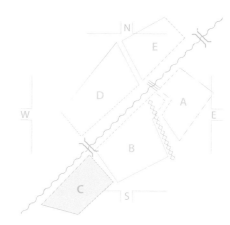

Gabon is a promising multi-ethnic country located in central Africa, with far-flung forest coverage. The pavilion, featuring representative African red wall and relief sculptures on the map-decorated exterior wall, depicts urban-rural relationship and provides an insight into urban-rural interaction.

Exhibitions, focusing on architecture, production, transport, culture and environment, display Gabon's changes and fast growth and its concept of complete urban-rural integration. Rural Civilization area presents its rural life, culture and the evolution of rural architecture. Urban Civilization area showcases its economic development, urban culture, urban construction and energy development. Natural Forestry Resources area displays the well-preserved animals, plants, landscape of natural reserves and tourist resources in its urban development. The wide use of green color is a good representation of Gabon's feature as a country of forest.

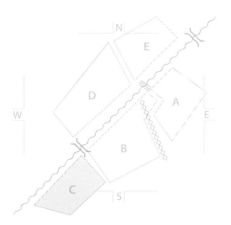

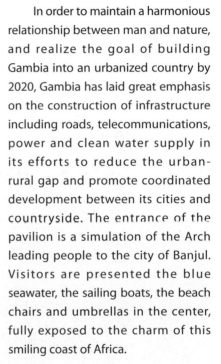

In order to maintain a harmonious relationship between man and nature, and realize the goal of building Gambia into an urbanized country by 2020, Gambia has laid great emphasis on the construction of infrastructure including roads, telecommunications, power and clean water supply in its efforts to reduce the urban-rural gap and promote coordinated development between its cities and countryside. The entrance of the pavilion is a simulation of the Arch leading people to the city of Banjul. Visitors are presented the blue seawater, the sailing boats, the beach chairs and umbrellas in the center, fully exposed to the charm of this smiling coast of Africa.

The area of Natural Life showcases Gambia's rich ecological resources, particularly birds, so that Gambia is regarded as an ecotourism destination and also as a perfect venue to watch birds.

In the area of Urban Life, visitors will be impressed by an exhibition on the world-famous Juffureh Village, the statue commemorating the liberation of the serfs, and World Heritage Site the James Island.

Ghana Pavilion

Theme
Garden Cities

Zone	National Day	Year	Month	Day
C	Day	2010	7	8

Like other developing countries, Ghana is faced with a series of social and environmental problems brought by the mass migration of people from countryside to cities. Taking "Garden Cities" as the theme, it aims to stress the importance of proper use of resources and eco-balance in developing economy and improving people's living standard. The pavilion is built based on the iconic building in Ghana, the Gate of Freedom and Justice, and traditional residential houses.

The main exhibition area displays holiday resorts, industrial development, herbal medicines, ethnic costumes and cloth artwork, providing visitors with an all-round image of the traditional characteristics of Ghana. The secondary area displays its balanced social development, proper use of resources, and new approach to urban construction, showing its efforts to build ideal garden cities.

Guinea Pavilion

Theme

Urban Development under Different Contexts of Environment and Natural Resources

Zone		National Day	Year	Month	Day
C			2010	10	2

Known as "the water tower of West Africa", Guinea boasts rich water and mineral resources. The Guinea Pavilion adopts local gatehouses as the main design element. A gigantic stone column in the pavilion gives visitors a sense of solemnity and solidity. Exhibits such as sculptures, murals and handicrafts with distinctive folk characteristics, as well as pictures and movies, are presented to showcase its history and culture, diversified natural environment and ample resources from different perspectives, and shed light on the ways to balance resource exploitation and urban development, in a bid to advance urban development on the basis of environmental protection. The pavilion shows with multimedia how the country tackles problems such as urban economic development, ecological conservation, migration from rural areas to cities as well as poverty issues.

上海
世博会

Guinea-Bissau Pavilion

Urbanization, Environment and Sustainable Development

Zone	National Day	Year	Month	Day
C		2010	9	24

Guinea-Bissau is located in Western Africa with ample sunshine and great biodiversity. The pavilion is divided into four exhibition areas, i.e. Urban Resources, Scenery, Culinary Culture, and Folk Show. It showcases the life of city dwellers of Guinea-Bissau in the past, at present and in the future. The challenges facing the country and possible solutions are also presented. The pavilion envisions a bright future as follows: people live in ecological, healthy, safe and livable cities, and all have access to natural resources and social services; in such a society, sustainable development will become a reality. In the center of the pavilion, featured performances from Guinea-Bissau are put on stage. In the Food section, visitors are able to savor Guinea-Bissau style cuisine while appreciating the pictures and videos about the country's culture and natural sceneries.

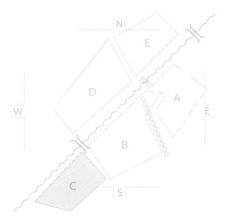

上海
世博会

Kenya, lying at the equator in East Africa, is a multi-ethnic country with topographic diversity. The pavilion is a Kenyan-style building with the application of murals, music and dance. The exhibition showcases Kenya's unique urban styles, highlighting the harmony between city and nature as well as the problems in urban development.

The pavilion has four exhibition areas. The Manyatta area presents various Kenyan-style performances and typical daily activities in Maasai culture. The National Park area shows how to protect wild animals in the urban development of Nairobi. The New City of Nairobi area presents Nairobi's characteristics as a regional center with its unique architectural elements. The Old City of Lamu area presents how Lamu adapts to the ever-changing external environment.

Lesotho Pavilion

Theme

Tradition and Modern Cities

Zone	National Day	Year	Month	Day
C		2010	10	4

EXPO
2010

Lesotho is a landlocked and mountainous country in the Southeast Africa. Its pavilion incorporates countryside cottages and a central plaza, demonstrating the integration of traditional Lesotho culture into modern cities.

A group of characteristic Basotho cottages in the center, with stone-and-earth walls, thatch roofs and traditional kitchens and utensils displayed inside, depict scenes of country life and symbolise the central role of rural communities in Basotho culture. In the centre of the largest cottage stands a life-size sculpture of a Basotho couple in traditional costumes. The information walls present the unique sceneries and architectural styles in different regions of the country. The central plaza allows for free communication, and introduces the country's history, culture and economy, especially its experience of increasing added value of local resources and creating employment opportunities.

Liberia Pavilion

Unlike most African countries, Liberia is well-known for its plentiful rainfall. Using "water" as an elemental trace, the pavilion presents a nation with favorable geographical location, beautiful natural environment and ingenious people, showing Liberia's readiness for renaissance, happiness for regaining peace, and confidence in the future.

There are three exhibition areas. Liberia in Rain area displays Liberia's unique landscapes, picturesque sceneries, and its history. People's Life area showcases how Liberian people use water effectively in daily life. Power of Women area shows how President Ellen Johnson-Sirleaf led Liberians in ending the war and starting a new epoch in the country's history.

Madagascar Pavilion

Theme

Living Naturally:
Diversified Ecology–Culture–
Development– Tourism

Zone	National	Year	Month	Day
C	Day	2010	5	30

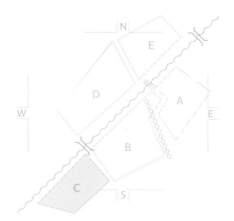

Madagascar is a country with the largest number of endemic plants and animal species. Modernization has had little impact on its ecological environment. Ancient cultural heritage coexists with modernization and globalization. Madagascar Pavilion is dedicated to showing the country's distinctive landscape, the varied climate, culture, and the modernized lifestyle in cities and peripheral countryside.

The pavilion is divided into three exhibition areas. In frontal area, a large HD screen introduces the philosophy of enjoying nature in a modernized world. The lateral area demonstrates the Madagascan way of silk processing. And the pedestrian area displays Madagascar's varied landscape and botanical diversity. Leaving the hut and walking across a bridge, visitors arrive at the "city" of Madagascar. In just several minutes, visitors can experience both the rural and urban life of this country.

Malawi Pavilion

Malawi — A Smart Choice for a Better Life

Zone	National Day	Year	Month	Day
C	Day	2010	7	14

上海
世博会

The pavilion features gorgeous scenery: golden beach, serene lake, steep cliff, etc., all pristine and original. It is a showcase for the country's urban development concepts, unique achievements and practices.

Malawi's scenic beauty is reproduced through the Lake Malawi, the traditional boat by the lake, and conventional handicrafts with African characteristics, indicating the country's efforts in protecting natural and cultural heritages. With the exhibition on four cities — Lilongwe, Blantyre, Zomba and Mzuzu, the pavilion showcases the country's achievements in modern civilization, urban regeneration, cultural tradition, economic transformations, urban-rural relations as well as the role of cities in sustainable development and adaptation to environmental changes.

Mali Pavilion

Prosperity of Urban Economy

Zone	National Day	Year	Month	Day
C		2010	5	31

EXPO
2010

By adopting the colors of soil, forest and the Niger River, the pavilion showcases Mali's totem artworks, historical monuments and its unique urban culture which is nurtured by the brilliant ancient civilization.

In the Art Treasures area, visitors can see Sudano-Sahelian buildings together with Mali's modern sculptures. Mali Pavilion also demonstrates the production processes of Dogon dance's mask and other splendid handicrafts. In the cultural exhibition section, walking along the bogolan (a traditional Malian handicraft), the transparent blue calico and the batik fabrics, visitors can learn about the cultural essence of Mali. Inside a simulated Malian mosque, the production processes of Malian food and the culinary culture are exhibited.

EXPO 2010 SHANGHAI CHINA OFFICIAL ALBUM

Mauritania Pavilion

Theme

Paradox between Ancient and Modern Cities of Mauritania

Zone	National Day	Year	Month	Day
C		2010	7	19

Mauritania is located on the west coast of Africa. Half of the country's territory is in the Sahara Desert. Therefore, its culture bears both Arabian and African characteristics. The pavilion reproduces the architectures in ancient desert cities, and presents Mauritanian civilization with exhibitions on ancient desert cities and the modern city of Nouakchott.

The pavilion is divided into three areas. In Footprint of the Ancient City area, visitors can learn about Mauritania's ancient cities and the ancient civilization, including architectures, environment, mode of production and way of life. City Impression area is devoted to displaying the urban image of Nouakchott as a modern city. In the area of Urban Wisdom, visitors can see traditional tents of the desert area, and some huts from the river area. These exhibits showcase Mauritanian people's reflection on adaptation to the environment.

上海
世博会

Mauritius Pavilion

Theme

The Island City State

Zone	National Day	Year	Month	Day
C		2010	5	29

The Republic of Mauritius, an island state in the southwest of the Indian Ocean, has been striving to preserve its historical and cultural heritages. In the past, people of different races and colors of skin that traveled from afar to the island, faced up to adversities and took painstaking efforts to build a prosperous country. That's the main reason why Mauritius is called the "Nation of Rainbow". The interior of the Mauritius Pavilion is clad in blue and shows the physical features of the island.

The pavilion is composed of two sections. The section Colorful Islands showcases various projects which cover many aspects of the country, including history, biodiversity, modern development, ship building, eco-tourism, and cultural diversity. The section also presents the blending of diverse cultures, economic prosperity, and a brand-new nation that has preserved its historical heritages and assimilated different cultures. In the other section Traditional House, there is a traditional house surrounded by palm trees and sugar canes. Here visitors can experience the simple way of life in Mauritius and get to know how they have grown out of nothing and made miracles.

Mozambique Pavilion

Better District, Better Life

Zone	National Day	Year	Month	Day
C		2010	6	25

上海
世博会

The pavilion features primitive cottage and simple modern building, quite tranquil and peaceful in the picturesque setting of riverside woods. The exhibition presents Mozambique's urbanization and its ingenuity in achieving planned objects and sustainable growth based on regional development.

The four areas, i.e. a school, a traditional cottage, a modern residential building and a hospital, connected by the Zambezi River, display distinctive sceneries and culture of the country. The residential building at the front of the pavilion incorporates public project, urbanization, road construction and dam building. The school, a traditional rectangular building, focuses on Mozambique's efforts in education and culture. The modern hospital introduces science and technology in different areas. The traditional cottage sheds light on the country's tourism and hotel industry. And also on display are two key public projects: Armando Guebuza Bridge and Cahora Bassa Dam.

Namibia Pavilion

Theme
Experiencing Living Diversity

Zone	National Day	Year	Month	Day
C		2010	8	26

Namibia is a country in Southern African with red desert, green plains and blue sea. A favorable location has endowed the country with spectacular scenic beauty. Focusing on the sub-themes of Exploration, Discovery and Dreams, the pavilion showcases Namibia's traditional way of life, reform of its urban community and the protection of nature and wildlife, presenting a colorful Namibia.

At the entrance is an imposing elephant-shaped rock, which is flanked by a tall baobab. Visitors can travel through the beautiful Fish River Canyon and 11 key cities and regions of Namibia including Luderitz and Swakopmund. A small Namibian shed is set up for visitors to have a rest and enjoy delicious local cuisine. Pavilion staff are all Namibians with smile on their faces, making people feel like being in Africa.

Niger Pavilion

Control of Urban Expansion and Promotion of Urban Development

Zone **C** | National Day | Year 2010 | Month 8 | Day 3

Niger is a landlocked country in Western Africa, named after the Niger River. The process of urbanization has been transforming the ancient country into a modern one. In Niger, developing cities means to make proper use of all kinds of energy and resources and improve every urban resident's life. The pavilion, colored blue and yellow, is decorated with blue silver cross which is unique to Niger.

In the pavilion, City Pulse area presents Niger's urban formation, resources and residents to visitors, giving a full picture of Niger's urbanization. Cultural Essence area, featuring blue totem on white walls which is the symbol of local residence, displays cultural relics and artistic handicrafts that have witnessed Niger's history. Vigorous Living area presents Nigerians' daily life, agricultural production & stockbreeding as well as a variety of folklorist performances to visitors.

尼日尔馆
Niger

Rwanda Pavilion

Theme

Kigali City:
Heart of Rwanda's Economic Prosperity
of the Nation Reborn

Zone	National Day	Year	Month	Day
C	Day	2010	7	4

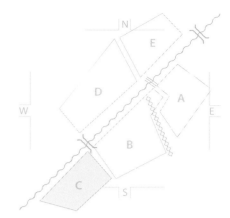

Kigali, capital of Rwanda and a 2008 recipient of the UN Habitat Award, has witnessed the renascence and prosperity of the nation. Focusing on the unique charms of Kigali city, the pavilion tells about the history and the future of Rwanda and its accomplishments made in slightly more than a decade.

The pavilion includes three areas. The History area exhibits fabulous traditional handicrafts. The Today area, a "thatched cottage" in the center, presents the image of Rwandan modern cities. The models in the Future area indicate the country's future progress. The pavilion boasts visitor-friendly designs, especially the kiosks where visitors can rest and look back upon Rwanda's road to revival.

Senegal Pavilion

Infrastructure Construction, Catalyst of Sustainable and Harmonious Development

Zone	National Day	Year	Month	Day
C		2010	7	24

As infrastructure construction scales up, more attention should be paid to the protection of natural, economic and living environment. The pavilion is designed based on Senegalese map and assumes the colors of the national flag. Spread above the pavilion is brightly red, hand-woven satin with wavelike patterns.

The majestic "lion" and the gigantic "baobab" at the entrance symbolize a country with both traditional and modern features and the harmony between mankind and nature. The pavilion displays the country's infrastructure, economic zones and tourism, handicraft and cultural industry through such means as display walls, exhibits and multimedia. Senegal's favorable environment for investment and its constant efforts in environmental protection and improvement are fully presented.

Seychelles Pavilion

Theme

Sustainable Urban Development:
the Seychellois Exception

Zone **C** National Day Year 2010 Month 6 Day 18

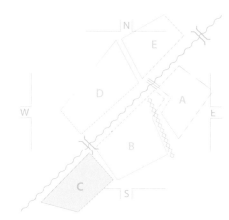

Boasting excellent natural sceneries and high living standard, Seychelles maintains its distinctions in the era of globalization. It is an island country in the Southwest Indian Ocean, hot and rainy all through the year. The pavilion, inspired by Seychelles' unique natural resources and cultural features, chooses coco de mer and granite as its main elements, and focuses on the harmony between the nature and cities.

There are three exhibition areas. In Spirit of Nature area, visitors are greeted by a vast expanse of coco de mer forest, a precious plant in Seychelles. The Land of Dream area presents the granite landform that exists nowhere else, a dreamy world with fantastic blue waves and light. In Balanced City area stands a spindle-shaped column symbolizing modern civilization, surrounded by spreading images of fish flocks, human smiling faces and Seychellois cities, signifying the human-nature harmony.

EXPO 2010

142

Sierra Leone Pavilion

Growth and More Urban Growth

The pavilion showcases the urban development of Sierra Leone and probes into the way of building a better city. Choosing orange as its dominant hue and huts, handmade carpets, stoneware and gourd-shaped lighting posts as its decorations, the pavilion presents an authentically Sierra Leonean flavor.

In the Scenic Beauty area, visitors will be impressed by the tourist attractions and mineral resources. The City Life area displays traditional living environment, folklore, handicraft and garments, accompanied with local popular music, bringing visitors closer to local people's daily life. Through multimedia, the Urban Development area presents the vitality of the natural harbor in West Africa and the development potential of Sierra Leonean cities.

Somalia Pavilion

Theme

Boosaaso:
A City with Unlimited Potential

Zone	National Day	Year	Month	Day
C	Day	2010	6	26

Somalia is located on the Somali Peninsula, bordering the Gulf of Aden and the Indian Ocean and lying on the boundary between Asia and Africa. As a transport hub connecting different continents and oceans, it offers favorable conditions for the convergence of civilizations. The pavilion features ample, independent yet interlinked spaces, blue-and-white hues as well as simple lines.

The exhibition focuses on the city Boosaaso and its essential role in geological location and cultural exchanges. It also shows the influences of different civilizations upon the urban space and lifestyle of Somalian cities, especially Boosaaso. Somalia's distinctive civilization and landscape, practices of sustainable urban development, improvements in living standard, unique cuisine and exchanges with other countries are all displayed here. In the Desert area, the camel models strongly contrast with the modern style of the pavilion.

索马里

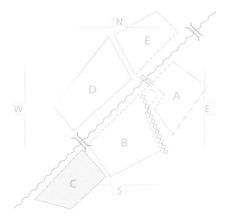

Sudan Pavilion

Sudan is known for its cultural diversity and time-honored history. The main entrance of its pavilion adopts Suakin Gate, a majestic and elegant Sudanese architecture. Combining traditional elements and diversified forms, the exhibition shows Sudan's history, urban-rural interaction and urban development, whereby highlighting the importance of peace to the country's growth and future prosperity.

There are three exhibition areas. Area I displays ancient paintings collected by Sudan Museum and introduces folk crafts, city scenery and wild animal protection in Sudan. Area II adopts multimedia to show the enchanting sceneries and historical progress of the country, especially the Sudanese people's pursuit of peace. Areas III provides a leisure place, where visitors can get finger nails painted with henna paste.

上海
世博会

Togo Pavilion

Theme
Prosperity of Urban Economy

Zone	National Day	Year	Month	Day
C		2010	8	20

EXPO
2010

Togo, which means "behind the shore of the water", is a country in West Africa bordering the Gulf of Guinea. Its capital Lomé boasts over half of the country's economic players and attracts the inflow of many Togolese from rural areas. The pavilion is a traditional building decorated with handicrafts that represent the culture of Togo like local carpets, canvases, rural-style masks and decorative sculptures. The exhibitions are to display the development of Lomé, its urban construction concept, the experience in promoting urban prosperity and problems encountered in urbanization.

Three exhibition areas are connected by circular corridors. Through the pictures on the wall, the pavilion tells the story of Lomé and interprets the theme of Prosperity of Urban Economy with real cases in beautiful music played by artists from Togo.

Uganda Pavilion

Located in the hinterland of the Sub-Saharan Africa, Uganda has a landform featuring plateaus and lakes. The exhibition focuses on Uganda's religion, culture, historic remains and environment protection, highlighting its cultural diversity, inclusive and harmonious society and sustainable environment.

There are three exhibition areas. The Mount Ruwenzori area presents the scenery of snow-capped mountains and introduces mountain gorillas, one of the local endangered species. On the bank of the Lake Victoria area stand unique red-crowned cranes. In Kampala area, churches, mosques, houses and colored wall paintings are displayed, and public traffic, wastewater treatment, environment protection and other urban practices are introduced. Visitors can taste the local drinks in the café.

上海
世博会

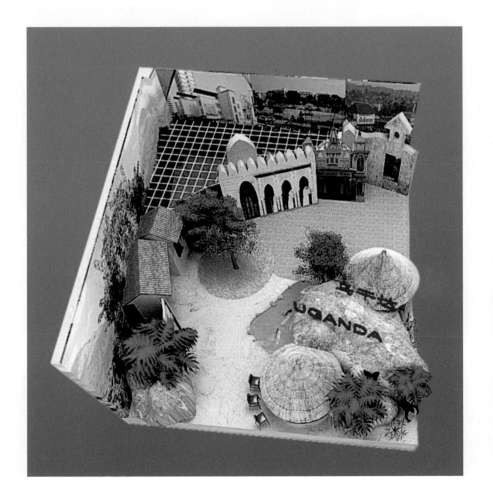

Tanzania Pavilion

Theme

Urbanization for Sustainable Development in Tanzania: Cases of Dar-Es-Salaam and Zanzibar Cities

Zone	National Day	Year	Month	Day
C	Day	2010	7	7

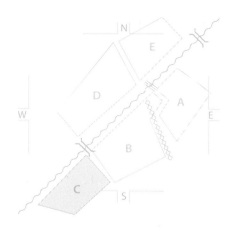

Tanzania is the largest country in eastern Africa, with rich natural resources, unique history and culture. Mount Kilimanjaro, the highest peak in Africa is situated in the northeast part of its territory. The pavilion takes the color of ebony and a modernistic structure with the antique grass-stalk eaves to show the harmony between man and nature in urbanization.

The central area features the sculpture of a giraffe—national treasure of Tanzania, and the movies of Mount Kilimanjaro, demonstrating the fantastic national parks and wildlife. In the two semi-enclosed areas on two sides, one focuses on Zanzibar Island, one of the hottest destination in Tanzania; the other is for important moves in the urbanization of Tanzania including community infrastructure upgrading program, reinforcement of safety of Dar-Es-Salaam, etc. The exhibitions in the two side areas unfold a picture of Tanzania's urban life, art and culture.

Zambia Pavilion

Enhancing the Quality of Urban Life in Zambia

Zone	National Day	Year	Month	Day
C		2010	10	24

上海
世博会

Rich in natural resources as wild plants and animals, with tremendous natural beauty, Zambia has encountered more and more challenges during urbanization, which can be countered by striking the balance between urban expansion and natural resources. Zambia Pavilion displays urban development practices and projects via waterfall, square and city model, inspiring people to think about how to improve urban living quality.

Visitors are to be attracted by the spectacular Victoria Falls; a large central screen on the Town Square displays the model of Lusaka, surrounded by four different types of architectures: a red brick residential building, a cluster of crude dwellings, a commercial building and a skyscraper. On surrounding walls are four key projects of Lusaka: construction of an industrial park, renovation of humble neighborhoods, improvement of transportation facilities, and management of water resources.

Zimbabwe Pavilion

Theme
Transforming Our Communities for a Better Life

Zone	National Day	Year	Month	Day
C		2010	8	10

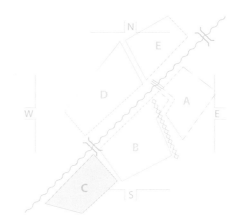

EXPO 2010

Landlocked in the South Africa, Zimbabwe is the only country in the world named after an archeological site. The word "Zimbabwe" derives from Bantu language, meaning "an honorable stone city". The pavilion is just a "stone" structure resembling the mysterious Zimbabwean cultural remains. Focusing on countryside and cities, it uses posters, videos and slideshows to exhibit the country's practical wisdom and unique civilization and explore the way of creating a better life through community transformation.

Every piece of stonework exhibited here carries spirits and cultural messages. The "Zimbabwean bird" perching in the center symbolizes not only the "stone city" culture but also the country's accomplishments in stone carving. The huge light box displays the majestic Victoria Falls and embodies the Zimbabwean people's ambition to create a better life.

The pavilion image is inspired by the incredibly rich culture of Algeria and refers to the architectural heritage of the Casbah. Exhibits and multimedia presentations together fully represent the traditional architectural style of North Africa and Algeria.

Visitors can walk through the "street" in the pavilion while watching the short movie of *A Walk through the Casbah*. Along the "street" there are arched doorways, and the large LCD screens shows Algeria's today. The roof is covered with images projected when looked from the top. A movie tells about the history and future of the country, embodying its determination in developing emerging cities. The section below the roof is highly abstract and incorporates the Algerian's imagination of the future.

上海
世博会

Angola Pavilion

Theme

New Angola, Bringing Better Life

Zone	National Day	Year	Month	Day
C		2010	9	26

Located in the Southwest Africa and near the equator, Angola has its highest temperature below 28℃ because of a relatively high elevation and Atlantic cold current. It is well-known for its abundant natural resources, vast forests and fertile soil. Inspired by the national flower, the pavilion looks like a blooming flower from bird's eye view and presents a brand-new Angola that is intent on bringing a better life to people.

With the help of modern exhibition technologies, Angola's natural beauty, history, culture as well as oil and diamond industries are well introduced via diverse forms. Visitors can see distinctive carvings and paintings. Through a water spray curtain, they can see a revolving totem made up of leaves, implying the indispensability of water.

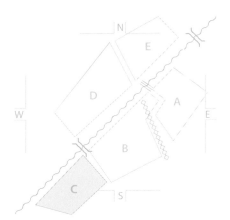

Argentina Pavilion

Theme

Bicentennial of Argentina's Independence: a Tribute to the Achievements of Its People and Cities.

Zone	National Day	Year	Month	Day
C		2010	6	10

The year 2010 witnesses the bicentennial of Argentina's independence. The pavilion, divided into an outdoor and an indoor area, uses photos, traditional articles and multimedia presentations to show the country's pursuit of sustainable urbanization and its achievements in cultural and urban development in the past two centuries.

The exhibition highlights the diverse cultures of Argentina as a country of immigrants and its efforts in historical heritage preservation, technological innovation, urban development and offering quality life for its urban residents. The pavilion also depicts future cities in Argentina, presenting its cultural essence, environment programs and technology plans, etc. Besides, people can enjoy passionate tango shows popular in the country.

上海
世博会

Austria Pavilion

Theme
Austrian — Feel the Harmony

Zone	National Day	Year	Month	Day
C		2010	5	21

By providing a virtual platform, the pavilion displays distinctive Austrian sceneries and its charms, tells about major events in the country's economic and cultural fields and shows its people's quality life, interpreting the theme of harmony from various angles. With a shape of lying guitar and curved interior wall, the pavilion adopts porcelain in its exterior wall and interior decorations, which symbolizes the return of this important export from China to Europe since the Middle Ages.

Roaming through the five areas, visitors can take a fantastic journey from snow-capped mountains, forests and flowing rivers to cityscape and experience the "urban-rural interaction". Sixty-four overhead projectors and millions of slides make a feast of sensory delights. Visitors can "throw snowballs", "listen to songs of birds" and come across "squirrels" rushing under their feet. They can also enjoy the classic works by Strauss and Mozart as well as Austrian country music and join in avant-garde music shows and parties.

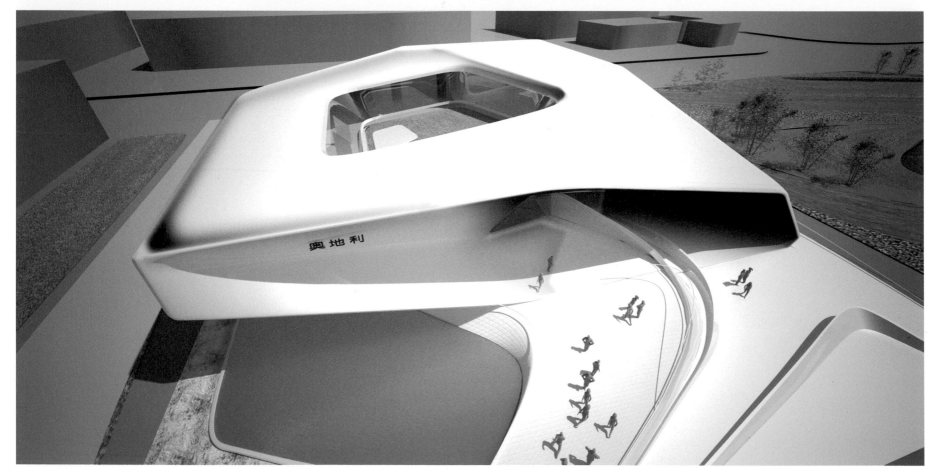

Belarus Pavilion

Theme

Culture Diversity in the City; Economic Well-being in the City; Scientific and Technical Innovations in the City; Improvement of Living Condition; Urbanization

Zone	National Day	Year	Month	Day
C		2010	10	11

Belarus is a landlocked country on the western plains of Eastern Europe. Multiple means are used to show Belarus' achievements in urban development and its efforts to create a comfortable inhabitancy in cities by improving cultural diversity, economic well-being, technical innovations and living conditions.

Exhibition of historical and cultural heritage in Minsk, reconstructed after WWII, is to show how much the capital city values peace and hates wars. Wildlife, eco-tourism and other exhibition items are to showcase Belarus' experience in promoting urban-rural interaction.

上海
世博会

Belgium-EU Pavilion

Theme of Belgium Pavilion

Movement and Interaction

Theme of EU Pavilion

A European Intelligence

Zone	Belgium	Year	Month	Day
C	National Day	2010	6	13

The pavilion is created around the structure of a "Brain Cell", evoking the artistic richness of Belgium and Europe, as well as their contributions to the development and enrichment of culture. It also refers to the role of Belgium as one of Europe's main gathering centers and cross-points of three great cultural traditions. In contrast to the simple yet elegant colors of the exterior, the interior design is innovative and fascinating.

A dreamlike "chocolate factory" is reproduced in which visitors can see the making of chocolate. Some of these chocolates are in the shape of landmark buildings in Shanghai. Besides, diamond designers from all over the world bring their works to stage a top-class diamond show.

Belgium holds the Presidency of the European Union in the second half of 2010. About 1 000 m² of the pavilion is offered to the EU for exhibition, presenting EU's past, present, policies and achievements.

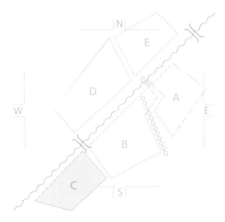

Bosnia and Herzegovina Pavilion

Theme
Whole Country — One City

Zone	National Day	Year	Month	Day
C		2010	5	9

The pavilion, like a castle in fairy-tales, integrates children's dreams and city images in its design. Its exterior wall is decorated with children's drawings and the theme logo Whole Country — One City standing out on the facade. In the pavilion, a ramp in the shape of figure "8" winds through the central space, along which are different sections for exhibitions on culture, economy, technology, community remodeling and urban-rural interaction, presenting the nation's spirits, lifestyle and unique concept of cities.

The Central Urban Space area introduces the local folklore by means of city models, puppet shows and performances, and the Natural Space area presents Mediterranean fortresses, buildings and citizens' daily life. In the Cinema and the Interaction area, visitors are bound to be charmed by the country's magnificent sceneries, learn about its culture and history and feel its spirits. The exhibition in the Urban Innovation area highlights successful cases which embody the importance of "cooperation, experience and sharing".

上海
世博会

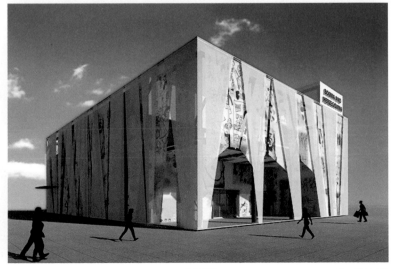

Brazil Pavilion

Theme
Pulsing Cities: Feel the Life of Brazilian Cities

Zone	National Day	Year	Month	Day
C		2010	6	3

Shaped like the Bird's Nest, the pavilion's exterior is covered by recyclable intersecting wooden laces. The sections and themed corridors in the pavilion show the charming and dynamic cities in Brazil.

The plasma display panel in the pavilion presents Brazilian mountains, flowers and birds. A TV wall, made up of more than a hundred of LCDs, displays Brazil's urban landscape. The panoramic stage, composed of four cubic screens in the central section, show the downtown area in Brazilian cities with strong visual impact. The dynamism and vitality of Brazil is also displayed by Samba and Bossa nova. Besides, visitors have chances to meet popular Brazilian football players.

Canada Pavilion

Canada is experienced in developing cities that are characterized by social inclusion, sustainability and creativity, and offer a high-quality life for residents. "Inclusive Cities" reflect Canada's cultural diversity and respect for the equality and rights of individuals; "Sustainable Cities" strive to strike a balance between the needs of people and the environment; "Creative Cities" are modern hubs of innovation and creativity where talent and knowledge are highly valued. The pavilion is anchored by an open public place and surrounded by three large structures. It is shaped like a large letter C, the initial of Canada.

The pavilion with an open public plaza as the center showcases Canada's rich resources and picturesque scenes and puts on a wide range of colorful cultural programs, especially Canada's works of art, brilliant performances and interactive exhibition. Cirque du Soleil puts on spectacular acrobatics show. Visitors can ride a bike in front of a huge 3D screen, feeling as if traveling in Canada. The simulated waterfall varies its flow with different movements of the visitors.

上海
世博会

Caribbean Community Joint Pavilion

Caribbean Community Joint Pavilion encompasses the exhibitions of Antigua and Barbuda, Bahamas, Barbados, Belize, Caribbean Community, Caribbean Development Bank, Dominica, Grenada, Guyana, Haiti, Jamaica, Saint Kitts and Nevis, Saint Lucia, Saint Vincent and the Grenadines, Suriname, and Trinidad and Tobago.

EXPO
2010

Antigua and Barbuda Pavilion

Theme

The Beach Is Just the Beginning

Zone
C

National Day

Year
2010

Month
7

Day
17

Antigua is famous for its beach, international rowing competition and carnival, and the numerous wild animals in Barbuda attract tourists from across the world. The pavilion, consisting of an openwork roof and simple columns, presents the country's lifestyle and future urban development.

The pavilion is divided into Turtle Bay, Fallow Deer Drive and Black Pineapple Court. Exhibits, events and interactions introduce the culture, history and lifestyle of the country. Visitors can know more about the country through touch-screen devices and take photos in the displayed costume. A museum of traditional Sugar Mills is set in Fallow Deer Drive to tell their history and latest development. Black Pineapple Court is crowded by tropical plants, and there is a movie telling about the country's today.

上海
世博会

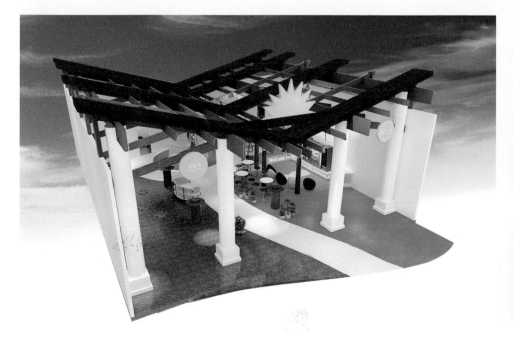

Bahamas Pavilion

Zone **C**   National Day   Year 2010   Month 7   Day 17

Bahamas has pleasant climate, rich fishery resources, developed shipping services and enchanting seascape. Beach mural on a partial side wall, artificial coconut trees and white sandy beach constitute a typical seascape of Bahamas. Multi-faceted exhibitions interpret fully its natural landscape, culture, and urban development.

The pavilion is designed in the form of two large sailing sloops connected at the back by an open gallery and separated by a central foyer whose floor features a map of the country. A mural is displayed on the wall to depict the past, present and future of capital city Nassau. Still images of underwater scenery, hotels, weddings, historic landmarks and video on Junkanoo Parade are displayed on the big screen, enriching the image of Bahamas.

Barbados Pavilion

Blending Diverse Cultures in the City

Zone	National Day	Year	Month	Day
C		2010	7	17

Barbados is known as the "Sanatorium of the West Indies" for its beautiful beaches, ports and parks as well as rich sunshine and agreeable climate. The three pillars of its economy are tourism, sugarcane farming and sugar manufacturing.

Various means including objects, models, and photos are used in the exhibition to show its natural landscape, developed economy and rich culture.

The exhibition is to show the unique charm of Barbados.

Skateboard surfing and submarine touring, most favorite among tourists, are showcased to arouse visitors' interest in the country, in addition to its unique sugar cane culture.

上海
世博会

Belize Pavilion

Zone	National Day	Year	Month	Day
C	Day	2010	7	17

Belize, which used to be one of the main settlements for the Mayan, boasts an ancient history and brilliant culture as well as unique scenery and various resources. Its Blue Hole is one of the most coveted diving sites in the world. "Palm trees" at the entrance are evocative of island landscape.

EXPO
2010

Belize Blue Hole tells the history of Belize and arouses the curiosity and imagination of visitors. The three sections, Forest Products, Mayan Relics and Marine Products, display the country's marvelous beach scenes, rich natural resources and unique culture. The Mayan Relics section highlights Belize's cultural tradition and carving technique. The Forest Products section exhibits specimens of Belize's forest creatures and projection of forest scenes. Belize's marine life and local customs are reproduced on the splendid blue background wall.

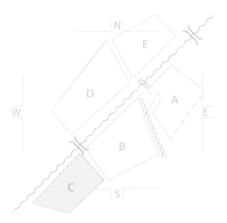

Caribbean Community Pavilion

Theme

Many Islands, Different Experiences

Zone	Honor Day	Year	Month	Day
C		2010	7	17

Founded in 1973, Caribbean Community is a regional organization of 15 members for economic cooperation whose secretariat is based in Georgetown, Guyana. It aims to promote economic integration and cooperation between member states. The pavilion, with a special appearance and artful layout, aims to display the unique natural landscape and economic achievements of the organization's 15 members.

A rich Caribbean ambiance is created by the exhibition of typical island scenery, a busy modern port, exquisite crafts, and children's bright smiles. Joyful and passionate Junkanoo parades depict the historical and cultural landscape of Bahamians. Straw-woven crafts are attractive to all visitors.

上海
世博会

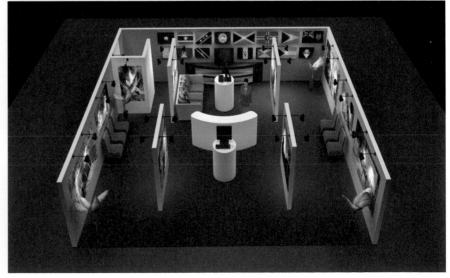

Caribbean Development Bank Pavilion

Theme
Promoting a Better Life for the Caribbean People

Zone	Honor Day	Year	Month	Day
C	Day	2010	7	17

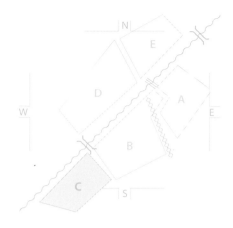

Officially founded in 1970 and headquartered in Bridgetown, capital city of Barbados, CDB facilitates coordinated economic development, cooperation and integration in Caribbean region and provides loans and assistance to the developing countries there. The pavilion with a plain style showcases the past, present and future of the Bank as well as its contribution to regional economic, social and urban development.

Images and videos with the help of lights in the pavilion showcase the life of common Caribbean people and local culture. There are also rest and business areas in the pavilion.

Dominica Pavilion

Dominica, facing Atlantic Ocean to the east and Caribbean Sea to the west, is blessed with rich tourism resources such as tropical rainforests, hot springs and cool springs. It is devoted to the development of green energy so as to create a green and harmonious country. The green roofless pavilion with integrated interior and exterior space focuses on Dominica's rural-urban integration and its development of and long-term planning for the use of clean energy.

The pavilion is divided into five sections, and such exhibition items as bridge, mini-windmill and cottage present the green urban landscape in the country.

上海
世博会

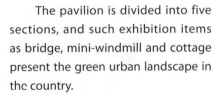

Grenada Pavilion

Theme

Rural-Urban Interaction

Zone	National Day	Year	Month	Day
C		2010	7	17

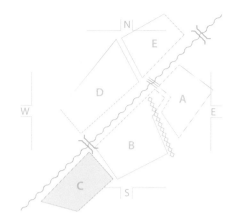

In recent years, Grenada is taking a pro-active role in adopting green and clean air technologies and demonstrating its commitment in being a responsible global citizen. The pavilion takes its form from spice plant nutmeg, one of the country's largest revenue earners and the key drivers of its socioeconomic development. The exhibition focuses on the urban development in the country and its experience in protecting rural tradition during urbanization.

There are long curved viewing galleries, necessary infrastructural components and a conference area in the pavilion. The display area in the red "mace petticoat" is for small chocolate products and carnival costumes. Besides, spice products, artwork of Caribbean style and Caribbean island scenery are displayed.

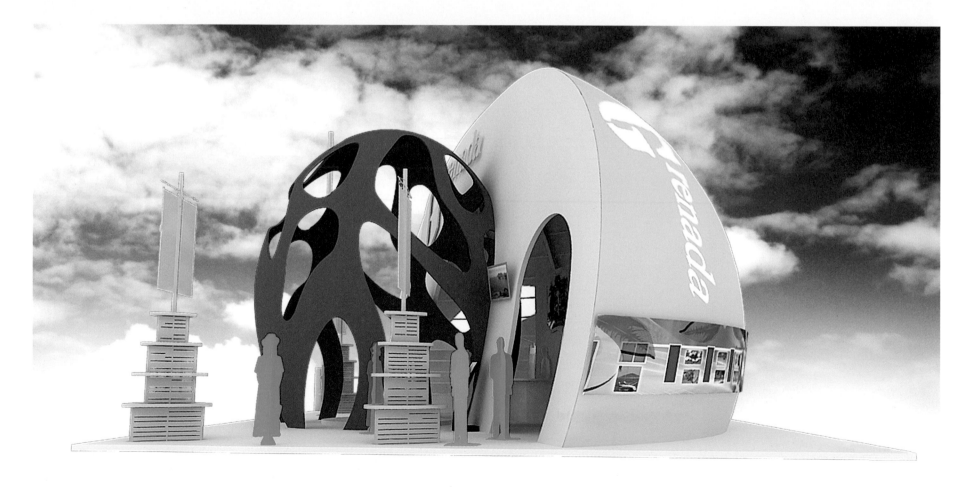

Guyana Pavilion

Theme

One People, One Nation, One Destiny

Zone	National Day	Year	Month	Day
C	Day	2010	7	17

Abundant exhibits in the pavilion share the country's development experience and innovative ideas, and envision urban development with visitors.

The pavilion is divided into The Time Tunnel, Guyana's Nature Wealth and Making Guyana a Modern State. The Time Tunnel showcases the country's abundant cultural heritage, the life of its people and its achievements in development. The famous Iwokrama canopy walkway, famed as Guyana's gift to the world, is the highlight of Guyana's Nature Wealth. Walking on it, visitors are bound to fall in love with rain forests and outdoor life.

上海
世博会

Haiti Pavilion

Theme

The Most Beautiful Island

Zone	National Day	Year	Month	Day
C		2010	7	17

The beauty of Haiti not only lies in its urban landscape, but also in the diligence and wisdom of its people. The entrance of the pavilion, whose design is inspired by Haiti's topography, is a heart-shaped graffiti area representing Haitians' vision for a better life.

Centering around "urbanian—city—urban planet", the exhibition is divided into three sections: People's Wisdom, Exotic Landscape and History & Culture. The People's Wisdom section presents Sans Souci, Citadel and Ramiers through pictures and real objects. Carnival in Jacmel, one of Haiti's most amusing cultural events, is reproduced to display Haiti's intangible cultural heritage and show Haitians' passion and wisdom. Visitors can also draw down their interpretations of Haiti on a recyclable blackboard.

170

Zone	National Day	Year	Month	Day
C		2010	7	17

Located in the northwest side of Caribbean Sea, Jamaica is the 3rd largest island in this region. The elegant and unique pavilion is like a maze with a small path winding its way and linking small huts, timber gates, corridors and partitions in the exhibition area. Yellow, green and black colors prevail, which respectively stands for natural resources and sunshine, thriving agriculture, as well as difficulties already conquered and challenges still to come. Palm trees and blooming flowers at the entrance convey strong sense of Jamaica.

Images, videos and models unveil natural landscapes, historical heritage and local customs of Jamaica. Visitors here may also have chances to sip the world-famous Blue Mountain coffee and its distinctive culture.

上海
世博会

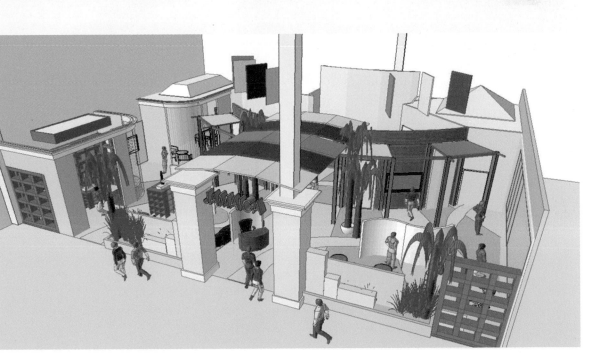

Saint Kitts and Nevis Pavilion

Theme
Urban Cultural Heritage

Zone	National Day	Year	Month	Day
C		2010	7	17

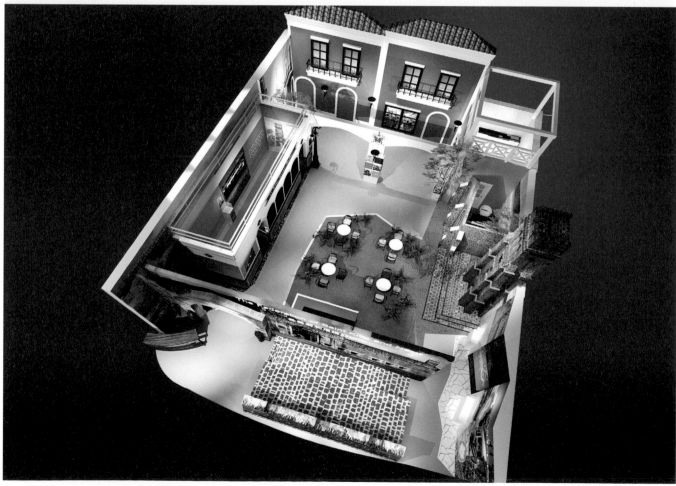

Located in the northern Leeward Islands, the country consists of such islands as Saint Kitts, Nevis and Sombrero. It has a rich and varied culture featuring its fortress parks, narrow-gauge trains, beaches, and cuisine. The pavilion is composed of four sections, i.e., World Cultural Heritage, Sugar Train, Carnival and French-style Capital, and Leisure Experience. Various means are used to display the country's experience in urban development.

Visitors can get to know more about Brimstone Hill Fortress National Park, one of the best preserved military buildings in Caribbean region. In Sugar Train section, visitors may be impressed by the narrow-gauge railway for the transport of sugar cane. Visitors are also exposed to the carnival scenes in the French-style Capital Basseterre.

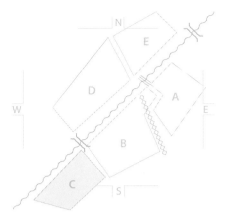

Saint Lucia Pavilion

Blue sea, golden beach and abundant sunshine, that's the stunning scenery Saint Lucia has to offer as a volcanic island with rolling hills, dense forests and fast-growing tourism. The pavilion consists of local traditional buildings, particularly two with steeple tops, and a large vivid picture of island scenery.

A variety of elaborate exhibits are used to depict people's life in Saint Lucia and to showcase the country's efforts in developing cities in a sustainable manner.

上海
世博会

Saint Vincent and the Grenadines Pavilion

Theme
City of Arches

Zone	National Day	Year	Month	Day
C		2010	7	17

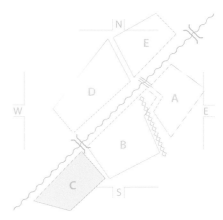

The country, consisting of the main island of Saint Vincent and the Grenadines, is rich in mountains, soil, rivers and volcanoes. Garden-style houses add a strong romantic element to its culture and tourism is a major engine of its economic growth. The pavilion is a simulated 18th-century brick and stone building with three brick arches and two antique lampshades decorated with tropical plant patterns.

Its interior, with imitation pebble flooring and simulated tropical plants, looks like a tropical forest. Galleries and video footages are used to display the rich tourist resources of the country, its culture and the charm of eco-tourism through unique landscape such as volcanoes, waterfalls, forests, and gardens.

Suriname Pavilion

Zone	National Day	Year	Month	Day
C		2010	7	17

Covered mostly with hills, low-altitude plateaus and forests, Suriname enjoys rich natural resources. The pavilion takes its shape after traditional Surinamese house and courtyard.

Multimedia and real objects in the pavilion present Suriname's brilliant culture and art, picturesque natural scenery and traditional urban life. The exquisite totem poles are sculpted by Suriname's outstanding artists. In the courtyard, sculpture of El Dorado is located at the end of the creek. Nobody has ever seen El Dorado, but the legendary golden mine does exist, which is shown in a video on the right side of the sculpture.

上海
世博会

Trinidad and Tobago Pavilion

Zone **C**

National Day

Year **2010** Month **7** Day **17**

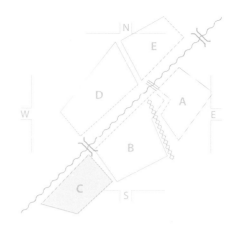

Trinidad and Tobago is an island country south of Caribbean Sea. It has a forest coverage of 50%, abundant oil and natural gas resources and the largest natural bitumen lake. The pavilion is a building featuring curves: curved gates, walls and partitions in the colors of its national flag.

Picturesque Caribbean island cities are shown in the six areas of video display separated by curved partitions and respectively named after major cities of the country such as Port of Spain, San Fernando and Chaguanas. Such a design helps visitors to see their favorite videos in quiet spaces. The rest area provides local drinks and delicacies to visitors.

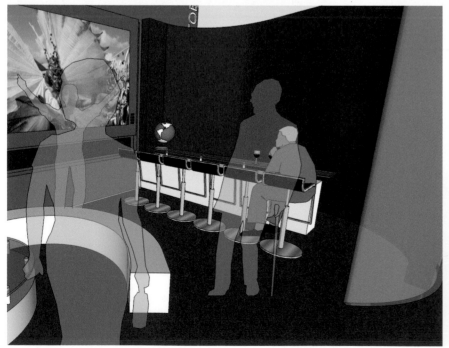

Chile Pavilion is intended to explore various social relations and tries to establish a brand-new pattern to improve urban life and give full play to the city's role as a bond. From an aerial view, the steel-and-glass building resembles a "crystal cup" with irregular wave-like fluctuations, inside which are Chilean understandings of the city. The cup is penetrated by a rectangular brown wood pole with its side end serving as the entrance to the pavilion. The U-form glass wall of the cup allows light in but is not transparent, and provides good heat and sound insulation.

The pavilion shows the development of Chilean cities and inspires people to think about the profound city-man relationship and the future of the city. Looking into the "deep wells" in the pavilion, visitors can see images and daily lives of Chilean people on the other end of the earth, implying that people from afar can be friends. A constantly transforming seed in the "huge egg" at the center of the pavilion symbolizes people's confidence in improving the city.

上海
世博会

Columbia Pavilion

Theme

Columbia Is Passion, the City Is Activity

Zone	National Day	Year	Month	Day
C	Day	2010	7	16

Endowed with favorable natural conditions and resources, the Columbian people are known for their innovation and enthusiasm. The pavilion is designed in white and natural wood color and decorated with butterfly patterns in red, blue and yellow responding to Columbian national flag. The exhibition takes integrated means to showcase the landscape, people, economy and cities of Columbia in the past, at present and in the future.

There are several LED screens in the queuing area to introduce the country and its pavilion. Models of cargo containers, unique buses and enclosing walls and castles alongside the Caribbean Sea are displayed to show the sceneries, industry and plantations in the Pacific, Caribbean, Andean, Orinoco and Amazon regions. The sustainable development of Columbia is further explored in the interaction area. In the store and the café, visitors can buy traditional handicrafts and taste famous Columbian coffee.

Croatia Pavilion

Croatia is a coastal country with beautiful landscape. The pavilion, with its steel-structured exterior colored Croatian red and dotted by white flags flying in the air. The pavilion showcases ways of living, urban development, and differences between inland and coastal areas, and ancient and new cities in Croatia.

Videos and images are presented by the 10 slide projectors on the interior side walls, displaying daily life of Croatian people in cities. Visitors may listen to the sound and music of Croatian cities. Croatia is the home to neckties. Featured neckties and shawls are sold in the souvenir shop of the pavilion.

上海
世博会

Cuba Pavilion

Theme

A City for All

Zone	National Day	Year	Month	Day
C		2010	7	26

Focusing on "equity", the pavilion presents the image of a city serving everyone. Different types of buildings such as Information Bureau, Havana Club Bar and Shop Cubarte form a harmonious public square, making visitors feel like passing through the center of a town. A multifunctional square represents the core of a Cuban city, and conveys the central message that the pavilion is to present, i.e., to grant opportunities on an equal footing to all inhabitants of the city, regardless of their social status, race, gender, culture, religion, ethnic group and intellectual level.

Assisted by digital media, maps, and brochures, the Information Bureau gives visitors the information of Cuba's geographical location, insularity, etc. Casa del Habano presents the classic Cuban cigars and historical development of their culture, carrying out live demonstrations. Local items such as handicrafts and music CDs are for sale in Shop Cubarte.

Through a virtual urban scenery, Czech Pavilion interprets the concept that a city itself is a fruit of civilization and highlights innovative technologies. The 63415 black rubber ice-hockey pucks on the white facade make a map of the old town of Prague. At the entrance is an elegantly designed spiral structure, inside which videos are played to introduce Czech, its pavilion and award-winning paintings by Czech's youngsters are displayed. Besides, the structure also provides people shelter from rain, perfectly embodying the idea of human-centered service.

The left display area includes the multimedia center and the theme hall, which introduce Czech's solutions to city problems; while on the right side, visitors can see a floating "city" on grassland, a virtual scenery interpreting the city-civilization relationship.

上海
世博会

Denmark Pavilion

Theme
Welfairytales

Zone	National Day	Year	Month	Day
C		2010	6	29

Andersen and his fairytales have won popularity among children and even adults around the world, making Denmark a land of fairytales. Like a fascinating book of fairytales, the Denmark Pavilion is divided into three chapters to portray happy urban life in the country. The pavilion consists of an outdoor and an indoor area which are united in one circle connected by a platform, resembling two overlapping sloping rings. The holes on the exterior allow sunshine to get inside; LED lights are installed in the holes for lighting adjustment and illumination at night.

The country's symbol and a world-renowned sculpture—the little Mermaid that has never left Denmark, makes her first visit to China. On the loop track, visitors can travel around by bicycle. A playground is designed for children. Visitors can also enjoy an ecological picnic here. The pavilion showcases Denmark's steadfast resolution and measures for environmental protection and sustainable lifestyle.

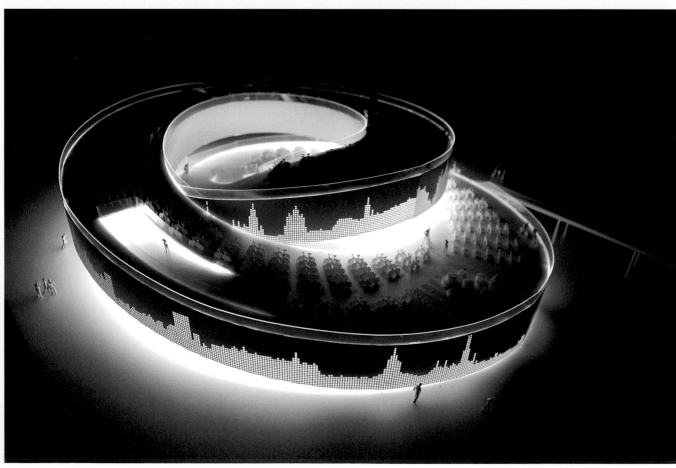

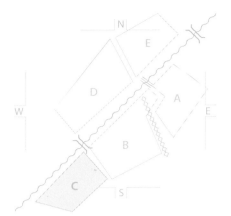

Egypt Pavilion

Theme
Cairo, Mother of the World

Zone	National Day	Year	Month	Day
C		2010	7	23

Cairo, a city boasting cultural diversity, has been embracing innovative concepts, different races and various beliefs since its birth, thus honored as "Mother of the World". The modern-looking pavilion, mainly black and white on the exterior, highlights the city's key role as a cultural center and its emphasis on diversity, openness, tolerance and harmony.

A great number of exhibits, movies and pictures are shown to introduce Egyptian housing and daily life, depict the sceneries of Cairo, and tell about Egypt's fascinating history. Antiques from Pharaonic times are displayed, accompanied with slides, documentaries and music that depict Egyptian urban life (tangible culture, folklore, rituals, etc.) and people's efforts for the development of Cairo.

上海
世博会

Estonia Pavilion

Theme
Savecity

Zone	National Day	Year	Month	Day
C		2010	10	18

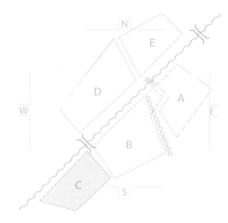

Decorated with colorful patterns of Estonian traditional costumes, the pavilion is a delicate fabric work highlighting the country's emphasis on green and sustainable development. Video clips about local customs are projected onto the interior wall.

The central elements of the exhibition area are colorful and interesting Piggy Banks. Every piggy bank stands for a positive urban subject, for example "for Fresh Air", "for Mobile Parking", "for Green Parks". Visitors may send wishes to their home cities as reference for city managers in making decisions. There is also a touch screen showing information on the country.

Europe Joint Pavilion I

Europe Joint Pavilion I encompasses the exhibitions of Cyprus, Liechtenstein, Malta and San Marino.

Cyprus Pavilion

Theme
City of Interaction

Zone	National Day	Year	Month	Day
C		2010	8	28

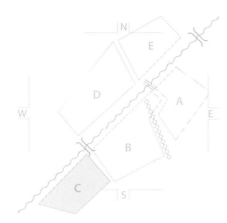

Cyprus, the third largest island in Mediterranean Sea, is at the marine crossroads of the three continents: Asia, Africa and Europe. Cyprus has been a fascinating destination for its bright summer and warm winter, beautiful coastal scenery and sand beaches, cultural diversity brought by East-West interaction as well as colorful customs. The pavilion, romantic and fascinating, is an epitome of the city of Cyprus.

On entering the pavilion, visitors are greeted by the huge mural of Aphrodite, glass floor with colored patterns of floral leaves as well as the feature movies projected on the wall. The movie *House of Aphrodite*, played in a 3D space in loop, depicts a miraculous journey from the past to the future. Exhibitions on the past, the present, the center and future are presented with interactive installations, videos, pictures and exhibits to showcase the historical and cultural heritage, modern cities and future development of Cyprus as the Island of Aphrodite, and illustrate the interaction between people of different cultural backgrounds, between natural landscape and built environment, the past and the future, as well as technology and traditions.

Liechtenstein Pavilion

上海
世博会

Liechtenstein boasts beautiful natural sceneries. Two thirds of the country is mountainous and sparsely inhabited.

A precious stone at the pavilion's entrance area introduces the country as the Jewel of the Alps. Valuable cultural relics, photos and movies are used to show how the country promotes urban development in the process of urbanization. In the pavilion, 50 000 Liechtenstein postage stamps form a classical painting of the landscape around Vaduz. The exhibition wall composed of dozens of large screens gives the panoramic view of the country with the help of special lighting.

Malta Pavilion

Theme

Malta: 8 000 Years — a Life Center

Zone	National Day	Year	Month	Day
C		2010	5	14

Throughout history, Malta was ruled by a sequence of powers because of its strategic importance in geographical location. The country boasts a variety of heritages created by the interaction of diverse cultures, arts, religions and architectures and is acclaimed as the "heart of the Mediterranean" for its unique charm. Nowadays, Malta has become a well-known holiday destination.

Focusing on "Malta: 8 000 Years — a Life Center", the pavilion uses sophisticated audiovisual technologies and intelligent lighting to showcase the country's history and culture, architectural traditions and futuristic cities. The most appealing would be various sculptures and giant rocks. An audiovisual room and projectors are used to present Malta's history, today's development and vision of a better urban life. In interactive area, visitors will get information on diversity, uniqueness and development trend of Malta's modern cities as well as the harmonious life of Maltese.

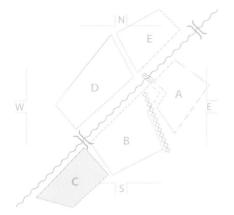

San Marino Pavilion

The City-State

Zone	National Day	Year	Month	Day
C		2010	6	4

Republic of San Marino, the smallest and oldest republic in the world, is a free and independent nation on a small territory with a history of centuries. San Marino feels proud of its past and tradition. The pavilion is characterized by a classical and modern style. In the center stands a replica of the Statue of Liberty, located in Liberty Square of San Marino.

Composed of such exhibition sections as Citizen's Values, History of Republic, Tourism, State System, and Video Wall and Maps, the pavilion displays San Marino's age-old history, major events during peak season and economic growth by pictures, documents, replica, movies, etc. The charm of San Marino as a tourist destination is well reflected in the elegant porch, corolla texture, multimedia presentations and virtual space. The exhibition sheds light on the key to San Marino's rapid economic growth: high-tech industry and stable financial system.

Europe Joint Pavilion II

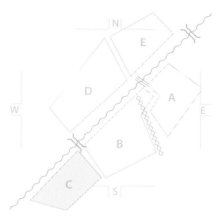

Europe Joint Pavilion II encompasses the exhibitions of Albania, Armenia, Azerbaijan, Bulgaria, Georgia, Montenegro, Moldova and the Former Yugoslav Republic of Macedonia, etc.

EXPO
2010

190

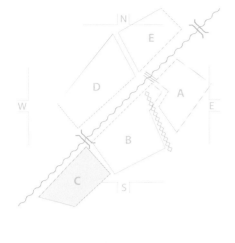

Albania Pavilion

Zone	National Day	Year	Month	Day
C		2010	5	5

上海
世博会

Located in the west of Balkan Peninsula, Southwest Europe and neighboring Adriatic Sea in the west, Albania has a long coastline and 3/4 of its land is mountainous, hence called the "Country of Eagle". It is a land of historical and cultural heritage and beautiful bays. Facade of the pavilion is a mottled wall resembling Albania's most ancient and characteristic city of Gjirokaster. Images of the country's landscape embedded in the archways present visitors the beautiful nation.

Images, models of historical architectures and videos are used to showcase Albania from various perspectives. The giant screen embedded in the huge "iceberg" and the globe-shaped projector bring visitors amazing visual enjoyment.

Armenia Pavilion

Theme
City of the World

Zone	National Day	Year	Month	Day
C		2010	9	21

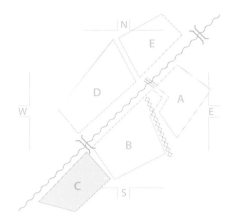

Armenia is a landlocked state in the southern part of Transcaucasia. Its pavilion aims to invite people of the world to construct the stable, prosperous and harmonious "City of the World".

In the center of the pavilion, a model of the "City of the World" is located, and a special scrolling news ticker within it displays information about online discussions of the project around the globe. The virtual 3D model of the "City of the World" is on display for all in the Experiencing Pavilion. In "Apricot Garden", visitors can embrace the blossoming apricot trees, taste the unique apricots of Armenia and enjoy the magical sounds of Armenian Duduk flute made of apricot wood. In "Gold & Silk", visitors can discover many interesting facts about ancient trade relations between Armenia and China, and get acquainted with the unique mastery of Armenian jewelers.

Azerbaijan Pavilion

Theme

At the Crossroads between East and West

Zone	National Day	Year	Month	Day
C		2010	10	15

The Silk Road was an interconnected network of trade routes and cultural exchanges between the East and West. It invariably crossed Azerbaijan, which is located at the crossroads between East and West. The Azerbaijan Pavilion highlights the important role the country used to play and its significance today as a still heavily traveled passage between Europe and Asia. The exterior of the pavilion is mainly colored blue and features a simple Euro-Asian style. With a color palette of creamy white, its interior adopts traditional architectural elements and integrates modern simplicity and traditional elegance.

Exhibits such as multimedia, handicrafts, and pictures, show to visitors today's Azerbaijan, and display how ancient Azerbaijan spread treasures, information, and culture between East and West through the Silk Road and its ambition to rebuild today's Silk Road.

上海
世博会

Bulgaria Pavilion

Theme
City of Shared Heritage

Zone	National Day	Year	Month	Day
C		2010	6	14

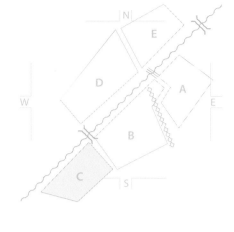

The image of the ancient yet modern country is depicted by linking past civilizations to present-day urban environment. Stone, glass and wood, combined in a fascinating way, are used to represent characteristic elements in Bulgarian architecture in the period of National Revival, which is the basis of the new style of city architecture.

Inside the pavilion there are two streets and a square, which highlights the change of urban spaces over time. Thracian gold treasures and mosaics of the Roman Empire are exhibited in the zone of Antiquity where archaeological tools are placed under the glass floor. The Bulgarian Revival corner, decorated like a museum well-known for its amazing murals and wooden carved ceilings, features unique architectural elements such as yoke, bow windows, big eaves and covered balcony.

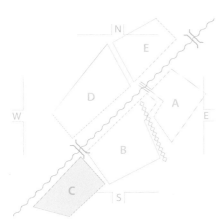

Georgia Pavilion

Georgia's long history and influences from both Eastern and Western worlds endow it with cultural uniqueness and innovation spirits. The pavilion resembles a typical "courtyard" in ancient Georgian cities. In the center of the courtyard stands a giant grape "tree", symbolizing the soul of city and indicating the winemaking tradition of Georgia, where people reckon wine as the symbol of new life, wealth and unique lifestyle.

上海
世博会

The four display alcoves showcase the country's historic relics, diversified cultures, natural sceneries and urban landscape. In the "Natural Scenery" alcove, visitors may feel like standing in a balcony overlooking the magnificent Mount Kazbek where Prometheus is said to be chained in the Greek mythology. Head ornaments, necklaces, crowns and bronze and iron statues made by goldsmiths in the ancient Colchis are displayed in the museum. Visitors can buy local handicrafts from the souvenir store.

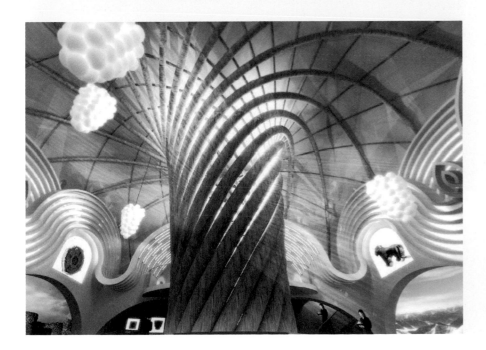

Montenegro Pavilion

Theme

Montenegro:
the Bridge between Civilization
and Nature

Zone	National Day	Year	Month	Day
C		2010	5	24

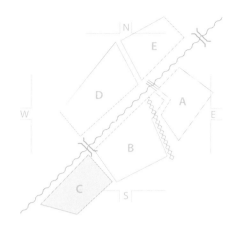

Located in the southwest Balkan Peninsula and on the east bank of Adriatic Sea, Montenegro is a mountainous country. The pavilion is designed based on the gorgeous natural scenery of Montenegro. The exterior wall is made of perforated triangular metallic sheets that are disposed to evoke mountains, and the colorful projections offer strong visual impact.

Various exhibits like forests, parks and coastal cities evoke the landscapes, time-honored history and profound culture of Montenegro. The pavilion floor is shaped in "mountains" which go up to a point that evokes the Mount Lovcen. Movies and photos are used to show the scenes of the costal city Kotor. Unique folk dances, percussion and ballet are staged on the National Day.

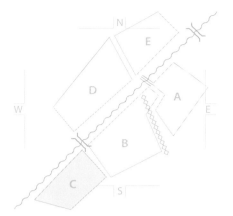

Moldova Pavilion

Moldova is a Country of Sunshine and Wine thanks to its natural environment and world-famous grape wine. Themed with "My City Is Your City", the pavilion presents the beautiful landscapes in Moldova through images and videos.

Highlight of the pavilion is an inverted pyramid-shaped video system in the center. Each face of the pyramid is randomly divided into small screens allowing visitors to enjoy different programs from different angles. Visitors have chances to sip renowned Moldovan brewery and wine. The rest area provides elegant seats in various shapes, which are comfortable, cost-efficient and aesthetic.

Pavilion of the Former Yugoslav Republic of Macedonia

Theme
Urban Continuity

Zone	National Day	Year	Month	Day
C		2010	9	7

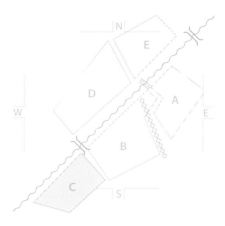

Located in the center of Balkan Peninsula, Macedonia is a mountainous landlocked country. The pavilion is an exquisite and cost-efficient structure inspired by beehive. It spreads the idea of environmental protection, energy-saving, and harmony between all nations in the world with beehive patterns in the design.

Images and videos about the historical evolution of Skopje from an ancient city to the capital city of Macedon depict the continuity of life. The interior wall is dotted with numerous pictures in regular hexagons about people's life in peace.

Finland Pavilion

"Wellbeing" in the theme indicates welfare services, technology, food safety and lively urban culture; "competence" refers to Finland's development strategy based on education, research, innovation and lifelong learning. Meanwhile, Finns are dedicated to applying environment-friendly technologies, so the island-like pavilion sets a good example of sustainable development, and conveys its pursuit of high energy efficiency, low emissions and environment friendliness.

Like a comfortable and inspiring miniature city, the pavilion incorporates freedom, creation, innovation, community spirit, health and nature into its simple but practical design, and translates Finland's natural beauty into a new form. There is a Santa Claus Post Office in the pavilion, where visitors can meet the Santa and send out a Christmas card or letter bearing his/her signature and the mark of the Arctic Post Office.

上海
世博会

France Pavilion

Theme
The Sensual City

Zone	National Day	Year	Month	Day
C		2010	6	21

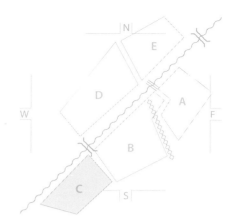

Romantic French people follow a simple philosophy that France is a sensitive world, whose charms can be felt directly. Therefore, enclosed by a meshwork made of new-type concrete, the futuristic building, assuming the shape of quadrangle, looks like a white palace floating over a stretch of water. In the pavilion, visitors can find French delicacies, courtyards, clear water, perfumes, vintage movies and thereby feel the sensibility and charm of France.

In the center of the pavilion stands an open-air "Versailles Garden" with streams and fountains on the water. The collection of much cherished masterpieces in the Orsay Museum, including six paintings by Cezanne, Van Gogh, Miller, Manet, Bonnard and Gauguin and the sculpture *The Age of Bronze* by Rodin, show visitors the essence of French culture; at the "French Romantic Wedding", a new couple take vows in the dreamy aroma of happiness.

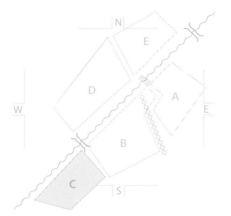

Wrapped in metallic silver membrane, the pavilion mainly consists of four irregular structures which are in a stable balance when interconnected. The whole building resembles a wonderful sculptural work, and an interplay of lights and shades adds to its beauty and elegance. The innovative cloth covering for the exterior wall can effectively screen sunlight. The harmony between city and nature and between innovation and tradition is explicitly interpreted.

Two virtual guides Yanyan and Jens explain to visitors about the exhibitions. Stepping into the Energy Source room, visitors are to be attracted by a large metallic sphere showing varying images and colors. The motion of the sphere and even its surface colors and images can be controlled by the audience who are divided into two groups yelling together. When it is stationery, it displays the images of the globe, sprouting of seeds and flowering of plants. "Harbor", "Factory" and "Planning Office" show typical urban facilities and people's daily life, and introduce impressive Germany-made products.

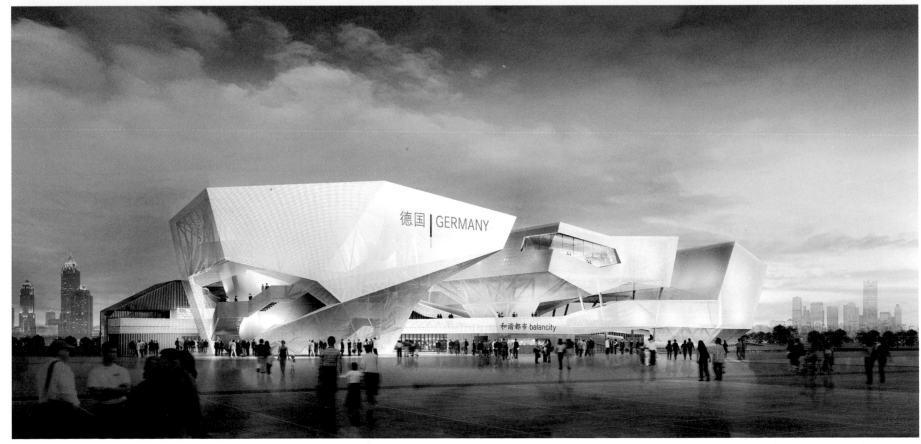

Greece Pavilion

Theme
POLIS, the Living City

Zone	National Day	Year	Month	Day
C		2010	6	19

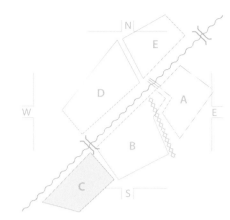

The pavilion addresses the theme of this year's expo through a human centered approach. Polis, (meaning "the Greek city-state"), constitutes "a city for living well" but also a live, a vibrant city! The design refers to the urban fabric, not as a physical replica, but as an interpretation of living and functioning in the city, as a reminder of the joy of urban life. It not only exhibits the everyday way of life but also reflects an insatiable thirst for living. Polis is well acknowledged for its livelihood and liveability, for the "anima" that it brings to its people and visitors.

The pavilion's uniqueness is that it condenses 24hrs in the life of a Greek city into the 12 hours that the pavilion will be open to the public. In fact, the pavilion can be seen as a "living organism" that follows a daily cycle synchronized with the cycle of the sun in Shanghai for the duration of the Expo. The pavilion's theme suggests the life style in the future by referring to the Polis of many thousands of years ago, which allowing the emergence of huge leaps.

Pavilion Halls include: Arcade, The City and the Sea, Agora, Ecology, Urban-Rural, Theatre, Living Together, Prosperity, Promenande & Port, Square (with café-restaurant and shop).

EXPO 2010

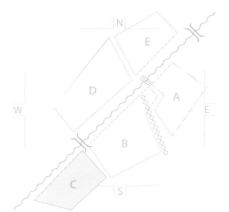

Hungary Pavilion

Theme
Architectural and Cultural Diversity of Our Cities

Zone	National Day	Year	Month	Day
C		2010	8	22

上海
世博会

The pavilion is a "forest" of 800 wooden sleeves. In its main exhibition area, a homogenous object Gömböc created by Hungarian mathematicians is to make its debut. The invention, similar to the Chinese tumbler, an easily tipped toy that quickly rights itself, indicates harmony and balance as well as the creativity, wisdom and perseverance of the Hungarian.

The wooden sleeves, arranged in uneven order, enable visitors to get close to forests and nature. They can give off light, and when pounded, produce agreeable sounds, which would vary in the morning, the afternoon and the evening. The sleeves, moving up and down to music, create superb audio-visual effects. A variety of works and Hungarian cultural events are shown in the pavilion.

Iceland Pavilion

Theme
Pure Energy, Healthy Living

Zone	National Day	Year	Month	Day
C	Day	2010	9	11

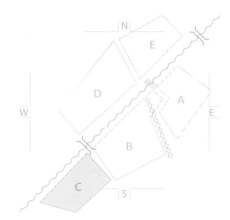

Iceland, located in the middle part of northern Atlantic , is endowed with rich clean resources (water and terrestrial heat), thanks to the most active volcanoes in the world and the largest glacier in Europe where rivers and waterfalls originate from. Its pavilion resembles an Ice Cube made of block lava on the exterior. Ice patterns sparkle at night when lights come on, presenting a magic crystal world. The pavilion focuses on the man-nature relationship, and showcases the wisdom of using clean energy.

With comfortable indoor temperature and humidity, visitors can feel cool Icelandic summer and smell flowery fragrance. Eight projectors create a 360° audiovisual effect; a short video shows the beautiful landscape and urban life. Visitors may have the chance to drink the world's purest natural spring water.

Ireland Pavilion

Evolution of Urban Space and Lifestyle

Zone	National Day	Year	Month	Day
C		2010	6	17

The pavilion consists of five cuboid exhibition areas. Connected by sloping passages and laid out on different floors, they are modeled on Irish cities in different eras, showing the evolution of urban space and lifestyle, and the efficient utilization of space and sustainable urban development in the progress of urbanization.

Stepping into the pavilion, visitors embark on a journey along the beautiful Liffey River, come across various art galleries converted from military buildings and take a sight at the urban traffic; they can also walk down the O'Connell Street, the first thoroughfare of Dublin, to witness the transformation of Irish cities and Irish people's efforts for sustainable development.

上海
世博会

Italy Pavilion

Theme
City of Man

Zone	National Day	Year	Month	Day
C		2010	6	2

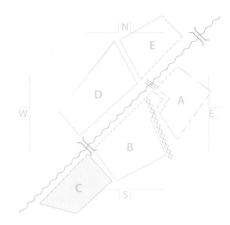

Italy, cradle of the ancient Roman Culture, devotes itself to pursuing its ideal. The pavilion design, inspired by children's game "pick-up sticks", reflects the country's persistence and its human-centered interpretation of the city. Consisting of 20 functional modules with each representing a region in Italy, the pavilion reflects the harmony of diverse cultures in Italy. A new material, transparent concrete, is adopted to improve lighting in the pavilion and create a dynamic and romantic atmosphere.

Exhibition of local customs shows visitors a country with a long history and profound culture; eye-catching Italian architectures convey the distinctiveness of Italian cities; famous paintings, fashionable dresses and sports cars showcase Italy's achievements in art, fashion and technology; Italian tailors, blacksmiths and violin makers present a city of vigor and happiness.

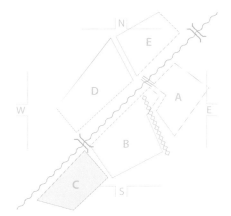

Joint Pavilion of Central and South American Countries

The joint pavilion encompasses the exhibitions of Bolivia, Costa Rica, Dominican Republic, Ecuador, El Salvador, Guatemala, Honduras, Nicaragua, Panama, Paraguay and Uruguay.

Bolivia Pavilion

Theme
Urban Communities to Live Well

Zone	National Day	Year	Month	Day
C		2010	8	13

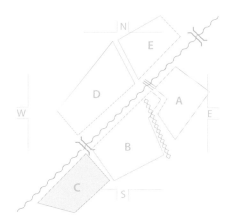

Bolivia, a landlocked country in South America, is endowed with rich ecological resources and diversified culture. Movies, interactive media, physical exhibits, and photos are displayed to interpret Bolivians' profound understanding of "the beauty of life": Flamboyance and innocence are the two sides of nature and life and highlight the world's diversity.

Exhibition sections include History, Nature, Circular Screen, Commerce and Culture. In History section, three touch screens are used to display the history of Bolivia. In Nature section, landscaping and multimedia are used to show the eco-environment of Bolivia. On the Circular Screen, a theme movie named *I lend You the Earth* is played.

Costa Rica Pavilion

No Artificial Ingredients

Zone	National Day	Year	Month	Day
C		2010	10	29

Costa Rica is a country in search of harmony with nature so it has identified as its objective tourism, business, economic and social development in balance with nature.

The design's portrayal of Costa Rica uses the stone spheres fashioned by the aborigines who first inhabited this land, also a cultural symbol characterizing Costa Rica.

Four themes are developed: Peace, Industry Investment, Education and Environment. Cultural performances, concerts with contemporary music, art exhibitions and cocktail receptions are held. Visitors can taste Costa Rican gourmet food and coffee, and watch the process of making coffee in the pavilion.

上海
世博会

Dominican Republic Pavilion

Theme
Intelligent Tropical Lifestyle

Zone	National Day	Year	Month	Day
C		2010	10	5

The Dominican Republic, a nation on the Caribbean island of Hispaniola, is a famous Caribbean holiday resort thanks to its beautiful island scenery. The pavilion is designed to integrate scenery with European/American-style architecture.

Photos and textual information are used to present from different angles the country's tourism and cultural activities, its economic development, innovation and use of technology. Passionate Dominican dances are also presented in the pavilion. The aim is to display the relation between urbanization and the improvement of living standard, encouraging a unique and intelligent tropical lifestyle.

Ecuador Pavilion

Cities and Historical Centers in Ecuador: Their Architectural Heritage and Cultural Diversity

Zone	National Day	Year	Month	Day
C		2010	8	14

上海
世博会

Ecuador, a country of biological and cultural diversity, has rich historical and architectural resources and tourism is an industry of major importance. Design of the pavilion's hemispherical dome roof coincides with the idea of "Round Heaven and Square Earth" in traditional Chinese culture.

Sections such as World Center, The Islands, The Coast, The Amazon, and The Andes highlight the geographical features of Ecuador and its unique charm of biological and cultural diversity. In The Islands section, visitors can see through special telescopes the volcanoes and various exotic animals like giant tortoises, flamingos and lizards on the Galapagos Islands. Movies on a circular screen show visitors a colorful picture of a happy Ecuador. Visitors can experience the unique joy that Ecuador offering through various folk games.

El Salvador Pavilion

Theme

El Salvador, Country of Volcanoes

Zone	National Day	Year	Month	Day
C		2010	7	20

El Salvador is a country of volcanoes in the northern part of Central America. Exhibitions on volcanoes display its time-honored culture, use of rich geothermal and hydroelectric resources, as well as its efforts to create a better life.

The pavilion is divided into sections such as Volcano, Coffee & Crafts, and LED Screen. In the center stands a huge "volcano" which has a steel structure, with special membrane structure and chandelier in the crater reproducing a vivid scene of blazing fame. Various crafts like pottery and cotton textiles are exhibited to show the simple lifestyle that Salvadorans have inherited from Mayan culture.

212

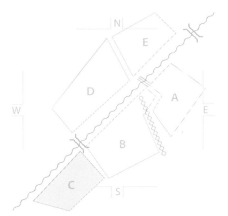

Guatemala Pavilion

Theme

The Mayan Legacy of an Eternal Spring

Zone	National Day	Year	Month	Day
C		2010	9	15

上海
世博会

Guatemala, inhabited by Mayan Indians in ancient times, is today occupied by their descendants, who are still making clothes and food in traditional ways and have preserved their cultural heritage. The civilization, achieving a harmonious development centuries ago, has stone pyramids, temples and sculptures, developed a system of writing using hieroglyphs and achieved a lot in mathematics and astronomy. It managed to use its natural resources without damaging their ecosystem, which is a great example of harmonious development and an important part of the exhibition.

The pavilion shows the history and diversity of the Guatemalan culture as well as its modern urban management and pursuit of future lifestyle. The recently discovered pyramid "Mirador" and dance shows are presented to visitors. Cocoa, coffee, sugar and spirit drinks, which are important in the history, life and trade of the country, are offered in the pavilion.

Honduras Pavilion

Theme

We Export for Better Future

Zone	National Day	Year	Month	Day
C	Day	2010	10	27

Honduras is located in north Central America. Copan, a small town in the country, is world-famous for the largest Maya Site, the religious and political center of Maya. The pavilion, in a simple and solemn style, is full of Mayan elements: two stone columns at the entrance resemble the statues found in Copan. A simulated red Mayan temple in the center bears patterns and reliefs of mysterious Mayan civilization. The floor is colored green and blue, symbolizing the coastal country of Honduras.The interior wall is sheltered by palms and bear images providing insight into the culture of the beautiful country.

EXPO 2010

Nicaragua Pavilion

Nicaragua, Unique…Original

Zone	National Day	Year	Month	Day
C		2010	9	14

上海
世博会

Nicaragua is a country of lakes and volcanoes in the middle of Central America. The exhibition displays from a unique perspective how much Nicaraguans love life after long-standing turbulence and how much they hope to create a better life for themselves and their future generations.

The Central Stage, surrounded by water, is green on the surface, resembling a small island. Simulated cascading and roaring waterfalls are presented in the Water Curtain section. A variety of traditional crafts and cultural events like music shows and folk dances are presented to show Nicaraguans' national characteristics.

Panama Pavilion

Theme

Panama City of the World, a Modern City with Sustainable Environmental Development

Zone	National Day	Year	Month	Day
C		2010	8	16

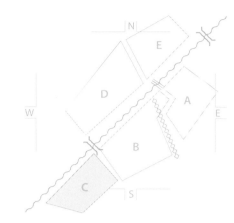

The Panama Canal joins the Atlantic and the Pacific. Its expansion, the clean-up of the Panama Bay, the greening of coastal areas and pro-sustainability environmental policy have all contributed to the better urban environment and quality of life in the country. Mainly colored blue and green, the pavilion features a simulated Panama Canal in a modern city amid blue sky and green grass.

Exhibitions provide a general picture of the ecological, geographical and cultural landscape of Panama and its efforts to build a better city. In Simulated Canal Lock section, a model of the reconstructed Panama Canal is presented where visitors can see the opening of the canal lock and the sailing of cargo ships. A water-curtain molding, composed of tempered glass and a water system, is to show the importance of its connection to the Atlantic and the Pacific. In LED Screen section, video clips about today's Panama are played.

216

Uruguay Pavilion

Uruguay is known as the Switzerland of South America for its beautiful scenery and also as Country of Diamond for its rich endowment in amethyst. The pavilion can be imagined as a square in the city center surrounded by beautiful landscapes, showcasing Uruguay's commitment to environmental protection and sustainable development.

Typical crafts, photos and movies are presented to display Uruguay's efforts to build modern, efficient, clean, green and friendly cities, to achieve sustainable economic and human development, and to show the quality life of its people and improvements in different fields.

Several artistic shows are held during the Expo, with Uruguayan artists giving original performances.

上海
世博会

Latvia Pavilion

Theme

Innovation City of Science and Technology

Zone	National Day	Year	Month	Day
C		2010	10	21

The pavilion aims to present the country's measures to offer clean environment and enhance living quality for its people through technological advancements. The facade of the pavilion is composed of 100 000 colourful, transparent plastic plates, which sparkle and sway in the wind, generating a dynamic, kinetic effect. The entry stairway of the pavilion leads upward in a spiral, symbolizing the continued, progressive development of humanity.

The glass vertical wind tunnel is the centrepiece of the pavilion. By participating in an interactive quiz using touch-screens, visitors can learn many facts about Latvia and may get the chance to win a flight in the wind tunnel.

Libya Pavilion

Tripoli, capital of Libya, located in an oasis on the northern edge of Sahara Desert, is one of the most beautiful cities along the Mediterranean coast. Distinctive Libyan architectures are displayed via modern exhibition means to show a city combining traditional and modern elements.

Large gossamer is used to simulate the changing sky from dawn to dusk in Libya. Narrow streets in Ghadames, scenes of Tripoli and buildings in Rome present an exotic picture with marvelous visual effects and enable visitors to better understand Libya's historical heritage and process of urban development.

上海
世博会

Lithuania Pavilion

Theme
Blossoming Cities

Zone | National Day | Year | Month Day
C | | 2010 | 10 25

Bud, the symbol of potential, novelty, and vitality, is the prelude to blossoming. Part of the pavilion looks like a bud just ready to burst, indicating the vitality and prosperity of the country and its cities, and that the dynamic Lithuania is looking forward to a prosperous future.

A progressing and vigorous Lithuania is presented in exhibitions on urban development, modern architectural trend, cultural heritage, environmental protection, sports as well as technological achievements. Inside the Bud is an auditorium and a moving stage. Petals are made up of shells. The circular screen and surround sound is to give visitors the feeling of flying above Lithuania. Handicraft artists give a live show of making pottery toys, crowns, wicker products, and woodcarvings. Visitors can also have a try.

Luxembourg Pavilion

Small Is Beautiful, Too

Zone	National Day	Year	Month	Day
C		2010	10	10

The pavilion is designed into a brown castle surrounded by greens, which echoes the Chinese name of Luxembourg: the castle in forests, and highlights the importance of the country as the Green Heart of Europe. On the roof covered by green plants, couches are placed for visitors to have a rest and enjoy the sightseeing.

A number of entrances and exits are available. Visitors can get acquainted with Luxembourg's economy, culture and lifestyle in the pavilion. In the 15m-high tower in the center symbolizing interaction between different peoples and diverse cultures, a cultural space is designated for real-time video communication between people in Shanghai and Luxembourg through satellites as well as a series of cultural and commercial events. On the open wing upstairs is a playground specially designed for children. Shanghai-themed stamps issued by Luxembourg Postal Office, and souvenir coins issued by the Central Bank of Luxembourg for Expo 2010, are worth collecting.

上海
世博会

Mexico Pavilion

Theme
Living Better

Zone	National Day	Year	Month	Day
C		2010	9	16

EXPO 2010

Due to growing urban population and buildings, the shrinking green space and public area becomes a major challenge to Mexico's urban development. The pavilion conveys the ideal of ecological balance and environmental protection and the hope for a bright future with two elements: green color (symbolizing environmental protection) and kites (implying development and freedom).

The pavilion features "a forest of kites", with all kites made of reclaimed plastics. The columns of the "kites" carry numerous pores spouting cool water vapor, and are equipped with interactive touch screens showcasing sustainable development projects in Mexico.

The three areas in the basement, at the entrance and outdoors, represent the past, the present and the future respectively, with the outdoor green space as the center. The pavilion shows Mexico's urban development, cultural heritages and local customs through the relationships between cities and nature, heritages and residents; a Mexican art collection brings a visual feast to visitors; and a European-style restaurant and a cellar create a romantic atmosphere for diners.

Monaco Pavilion

Theme

Monaco Past, Present and Future.
The Challenges of an Evolving City-State

Zone	National Day	Year	Month	Day
C		2010	10	7

Monaco, a country bordered by the Mediterranean Sea, tries hard to reclaim land from the sea and attaches special importance to protecting marine flora and fauna. Several blue lighted rings of water surround the pavilion, showing the close city-environment ties.

With a capacity of 250 to 300 people and a 56m² high-definition screen, the cinema plays the animation movie *Monaco, A Rock for Eternity*. As Monaco is dedicated to the world-famous F1 competitions, the F1 display area shows the evolution of car, city transformation, KERS system used during the race, and plays racing videos. Also on display are paintings depicting Monaco's history in the portrait gallery as well as an interactive globe installation and a luxury ecological car prototype in the sustainable development area.

上海
世博会

The Netherlands Pavilion

Theme
Happy Street

Zone	National Day	Year	Month	Day
C		2010	5	18

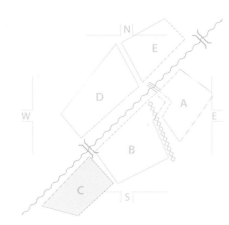

In a typical Dutch style, of being orderly, effective and practical, the pavilion shows novelty and uniqueness. It is mainly an 8-shaped walkway, along which stand 20 small elevated houses and a water purification station. The spiral street extends up to the sky, like a flying roller coaster tract. More than perfect shelters, the fifty orange umbrellas also serve for collecting energy and converting it into electricity to turn the pavilion into a magic world when night falls.

The winding door-less Happy Street, 400 meters long, allows for "street stroll" starting from any direction. With exhibits only viewed through windows, 20 houses fall into such categories as Living Section, Work Section and Industrial Section, exhibiting the ideal planning of modern urban life as well as the country's innovations in space, energy and water conservation. At the water purification station, visitors can get to know the purification process.

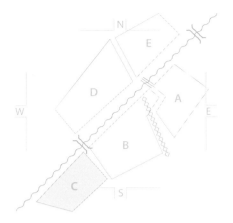

Nigeria Pavilion

Theme
Our Cities: Harmony in Diversity

Zone	National Day	Year	Month	Day
C		2010	8	21

上海
世博会

Nigerians know well that tradition and innovation should be balanced and local landscape must be protected in urban development so as to ensure environmental sustainability. Simulated Zuma Rock on the exterior wall, colors of Nigeria's national flag and simulated palm trees in the queue lobby create a Nigerian ambiance. Exhibitions display how to achieve the common prosperity of cities with different cultural and ethnic backgrounds.

A full picture of Nigeria is drawn through the exhibitions. In Bright Star of West African Coast, representative objects of ancient African civilizations and multimedia presentation are used to show Nigeria's cultural traditions. Today's Nigeria is shown in the landscaping with local tree species. In Rising Country of Harmony, e-maps, e-books, a big screen and a sand table are used to showcase Nigeria's diversified development now and in the future.

Norway Pavilion

Theme
Powered by Nature

Zone	National Day	Year	Month	Day
C	Day	2010	5	28

As most Norwegian cities are close to the sea, forests and mountains, Norway Pavilion invites natural elements into its design and bears a unique North European charm. Propped by 15 giant Norway "pines", it is decorated with Chinese bamboo and presents elegant and neat outlines; and the undulating "pines" roof implies a heartfelt gratitude towards nature.

· Entering the pavilion, visitors can first see the "seacoast" with two giant screens showing the country's natural beauty and highlighting its effective use of energy; movies about its urban planning, timber use and tree planting are played in the "forests" part; then splendid "fjord" comes in sight where water's crucial importance to man is illustrated via pictures; as an interesting end to the exhibition, the grandeur of "aurora" are sure to impress many of the visitors.

EXPO 2010

People regard food as their prime want. Given its critical role in promoting cultural diversity in cities and Peru's communication with others, food is the essential factor of the Peru Pavilion. The exterior of the square building is woven bamboo panels; inside, clay walls and platforms indicate Peru's traditional understanding of past and future. The two basic materials are most used in Peru's urban construction.

Focusing on Peru's contributions to the world food industry and various local cuisines, the exhibition also uses videos and pictures to present the mysterious attractions of Peru and highlights the urban evolution process. Renowned as home to potatoes, Peru innovatively portrays the urban food chain via potatoes, and calls for attention to the supply of reasonably priced, safe, convenient and delicious food. Visitors can have a chance to savor Peruvian food famous for its deliciousness and great variety.

上海
世博会

Poland Pavilion

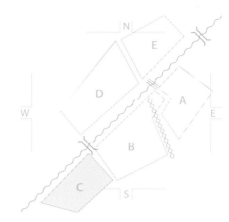

In an abstract and irregular shape, the building is unique for its paper-cut-like surface, translating traditional folk motifs into modern language. Thanks to the pierced surface, the beauty of light and color embodies the combination of tradition and modernism and also implies the critical role of people's creativity in pursing better urban life.

The flexible interior space makes it possible to use the wall as a screen to play movies about Polish landscape, culture, art and social life, to show inheritance and innovation in urban life. The Chopin piano concert held every day on the central square and in the music hall is to celebrate the 200th anniversary of the birth of the great Polish composer and pianist; special activities for youngsters are held every night where they can dance, sometimes to Chopin's music but in rock version; dragon dance show is offered in front of the pavilion gate every morning.

The theme was chosen due to the country's focus on "square" as a public space. The pavilion facade and interior wall are lined with the cork, a recyclable, ecological material. The entrance hall, colonnade, electronic screen and theme sections depict the history, culture, economy and people's life of Portugal as a gateway to the Atlantic.

The exhibition is organized into four sections. Pre-Show section represents the 500 years of "encounters" and history of Portugal-China friendship. A movie, *Portugal, a Plaza to the World* is screened in the Second Moment section to show the country's technological development; "Portugal, Energy for the World" in the Third Moment section presents Portugal's accomplishments in sustainable development and use of natural energy sources; In the Fourth Moment section, visitors arrive at a plaza called Portugal Today consisting of a café area, a wine tasting area, and a shop with Portuguese products.

上海
世博会

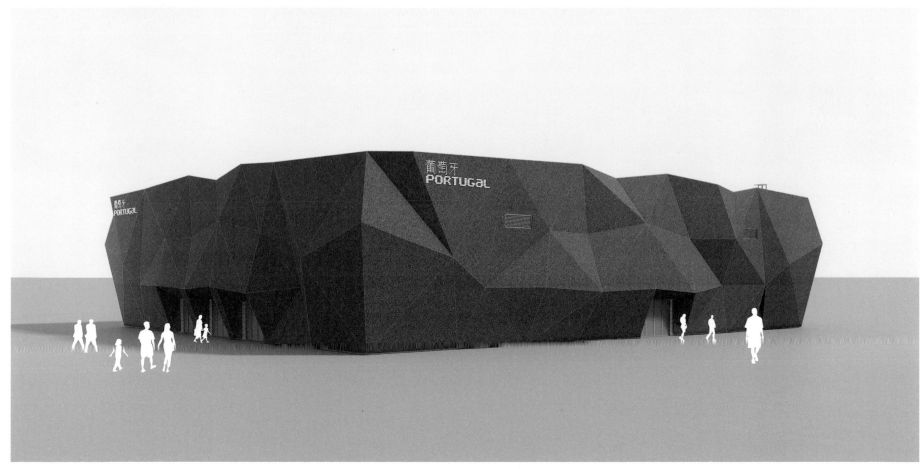

Romania Pavilion

Theme
Green City

Zone	National Day	Year	Month	Day
C		2010	7	29

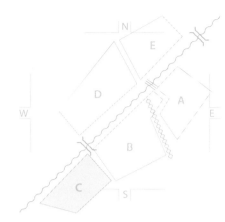

Also called "GREENOPOLIS", the pavilion resembles a green apple, the favorite fruit in Romania which symbolizes green city and healthy lifestyle. With exterior glass curtain wall and interior steel structure, the Green Apple can change into other colors at night and is connected with the "slice" with a white rain-proof film covering the roof.

Focusing on Millennium in Retrospect, Social and Urban Development Promoted by History and Nature and City life Close to Nature, the pavilion is mainly a five-storey structure. The most important storey is an open, all-weather stage offering folklore shows, distinctive performances and classic movies and showing Romania's fast development and modern civilization. Its "sliced" areas display Romanian history, urban activities and sceneries of Bucharest.

Russia Pavilion

The pavilion, a fairyland for children, resembles a sunflower or "a tree of life", and is inspired by the Russian author Nosov's ideal cities. Each of 12 petals is crowned with a tower decorated with national ornaments of Russian folks. The white-and-golden color can be turned to black-red-and-golden at night, symbolizing Russian traditional culture. The "roots" of the towers extend to the "cube of civilization" on the central square and form the shape of "人", meaning "man". The external components of the cube can be moved to create a huge "animated facade".

In the center of the first floor are city layout and miniature buildings designed from children's perspective, such as flying balconies, depicting an ideal city full of novelty and unlimited possibility. Also on show are a lot of Russian inventions. Both adults and children are sure to have a wonderful time here.

上海
世博会

Serbia Pavilion

Theme
City Code

Zone	National Day	Year	Month	Day
C		2010	6	27

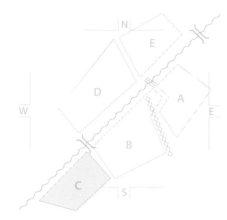

The pavilion shows Serbia's past, present and future and explores its urban spirit. Combining traditional Serbian architectural elements, the pavilion has a modern design. The colorful LED light on the exterior wall makes the pavilion extremely beautiful at night.

The pavilion is divided into a lobby, an exhibition area and a rest area. "Time" is a cohesive factor for numerous exhibits and events in the Serbian Pavilion present visitors the vision for a better urban life and better use of time. "Time Machine", made up of flywheels and belts, offers visitors magic experience of traveling through time. "The Face of Serbia" shows how Serbians make good use of time in urban environment. "The Garden of Europe" sums up the history of cities and the natural environment in Europe.

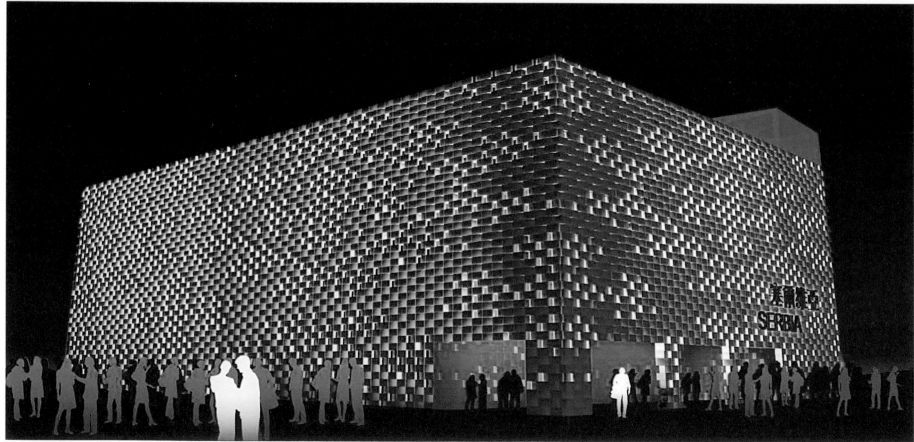

Slovakia Pavilion

Theme
World of Humanity

Zone   National   Year   Month Day
Day
C   2010   9   4

上海
世博会

The main element of the whole exhibition is a spiral copying the logo with the main letter "S" representing Slovakia. An endless spiral arising from the central letter is a symbol of never-ending eternal cycle of life and the creative power of mankind connecting the past with the future.

The S-shaped symbolic square in the center of the pavilion symbolizes that square, joining all roads of the city, Is a meeting point and the main witness of city changes. The square is surrounded by a wall with fragments of old-time memories representing historical milestones in the development of Slovak towns and architecture, telling about city's unceasing changes, movements and growth. The opposite wall represents the transition from past to present and future, and also serves as a projection screen to tell a story of city and its inhabitants. Besides, exhibits and performances show the country's unique charm.

Slovenia Pavilion

Theme
Open Book

Zone	National Day	Year	Month	Day
C		2010	6	24

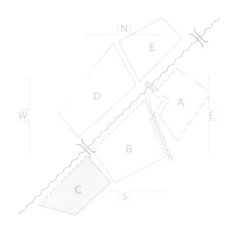

Ljubljana is the UNESCO World Book Capital in 2010, so its pavilion is themed on "Open Book". With a journey through open books, the pavilion presents Slovenia's city-centered development in terms of ideology, art and cultural design as well as its attitudes towards diverse cultures.

Facade of the pavilion is an attractive book shelf with thousand books on it. Once visitors enter the pavilion, the journey through open books begins. The eight huge "books" in the pavilion show Slovenia's economy, culture, technology, nature, and sports. Visitors can "read" each book through audiovisual means and wall-projection. By seeing projections and experiencing the sounds, temperatures and even smells, the eight "books" leave visitors differentiated dreamlike impressions.

South Africa Pavilion

South Africa, with a long coastline on the Atlantic and Indian Oceans, is endowed with beautiful natural landscapes and rich natural resourcs. The simple and chaste pavilion under a huge "umbrella". A full-color screen is applied around the outer central core to project images, sounds and features of authentic South African culture.

An "atrium" in the pavilion encompassed within wooden beams represents a traditional "Kraal" boma enclosure. Each South African iconic image recessed into the framework is accentuated by a halo effect, and the Zebra printed ottomans in the seating area enhance South Africa's aspects of nature. The bright finishes and furnishings in the pavilion represent the diverse cultures of South Africa and show it as an emerging country with a vision to create a better life for its people.

上海
世博会

Spain Pavilion

Theme

From the City of Our Parents to the City of Our Children

Zone	National Day	Year	Month	Day
C		2010	8	30

Focusing on the theme "From the City of Our Parents to the City of Our Children", the Spain Pavilion displays changes from ancient times to the present day, enabling visitors to understand the history of the country as well as the wits and creativity of its people. Besides, visitors are bound to feast their eyes on what excellent Spanish urban planners, sociologists, filmmakers and artists have prepared for them. Inspired by Spanish wicker baskets, the pavilion is designed to be a fascinating structure made of eco-friendly traditional exterior materials — hand-weaved wickers, 8524 wicker boards of different colors decorate the exterior wall of the pavilion;

ancient Chinese characters are pieced together with wickers to present a Chinese poem.

The structure is comprised of three exhibition halls: Origin, City and Children. Visitors can get to know about the true Spain through a variety of cultural and artistic programs, such as operas, dances, and music as well as the flamenco dances that integrate dances, songs and instruments together. A restaurant that could accommodate 300 people serves the most authentically Spanish cuisine. The pavilion also has souvenir shops, a multi-functional theatre, and a business center.

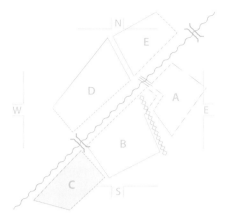

Sweden Pavilion

Sweden Pavilion conveys an important idea of loving the city and nature, innovatively countering challenges and improving people's life through innovation. It is inspired by the urban-rural interaction and designed according to Sweden's sustainability concept. The three-storey pavilion consists of four parts connected by transparent elevated corridors, resembling the cross on Swedish national flag. It is decorated with meshwork symbolizing cities outside and natural elements inside. If unfolded, the exterior wall is an artistically rendered map of downtown Stockholm.

The well-known fairy tale figure "Pippi Longstocking", as one of the guides, leads visitors to an amazing tour of innovation. Visitors are exposed to Sweden's culture, tradition, love for nature and particularly the spirit of innovation as embodied in its response to challenges, measures to improve urban environment and stress on communication in new technologies. Visitors can learn more about the Nobel Prize in a special area.

Swiss Pavilion

Theme
Rural-Urban Interaction

Zone	National Day	Year	Month	Day
C		2010	8	12

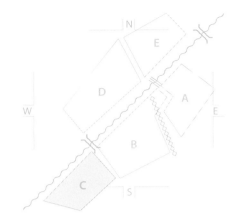

The Swiss Pavilion is inspired by the concept of balance, as embodied in the traditional Chinese concept of Yin and Yang. Switzerland has attached great importance to the urban-rural interaction due to its geographical characteristics. The urban setting on the ground floor is counterbalanced by the natural space on the roof and the continuous circuit of the chair lift provides easy access to both areas. The architecture embodies the symbiosis between cities and countryside, and emphasizes the perfect balance among man, nature and technology. The interactive, intelligent facade enveloping the pavilion can be triggered by light energy in the surroundings, resulting in a haphazard pattern of flashes.

Swiss people from all walks of life can be seen on 12 large life-size screens against the background of the Alps, talking about their visions of the future and responsibilities for environmental protection. Visitors may also enjoy the IMAX movie *The Alps* which shows both the beauty and harshness of the nature, implying that man and nature should be in harmony.

Tunisia Pavilion

Theme

Enthusiastic City, Connected City

Zone	National Day	Year	Month	Day
C		2010	9	19

This is a country with romantic and mysterious flavors. Its pavilion features a traditional archway and ethnic patterns, and the side elevation presents the enchanting sceneries of seaside and coastal cities, highlighting the significance of nature to Tunis.

Exhibitions include Country of Magnificent Sceneries, City of Diversified Cultures and Capital of Time-honored Civilization. Stepping into the "blue-and-white town" and traditional courtyard, visitors find themselves surrounded by flowers and music. In the amphitheatre designed based on Roman relics, movies on Tunisian sceneries, history and culture show the country's charms as well as its great tolerance towards foreign cultures. In the café, visitors are exposed to the Tunisian afternoon-tea tradition.

上海
世博会

Turkey Pavilion

Theme
The Cradle of Civilizations

Zone	National Day	Year	Month	Day
C		2010	6	20

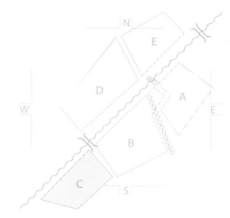

The exterior design of the pavilion is inspired by one of the first known settlements in the world, Çatalhöyük (the fork-mountain in Turkish). It has two layers of exterior walls. The first layer has expressive colors and makes use of an abstract image found on the wall paintings of "Çatalhöyük". The second layer is a fresco depicting hunting scenes and animals carved on the walls of the historic settlement which are now extinct. The pavilion displays a wealth of historical relics and exquisite artifacts that underpin the past of Anatolia as the cradle of civilization.

The exhibition is divided into three sections: Dreaming of the Past, Cultivating the Present and Aspiring to the Future. The multilayered stories of the past are fragmented into the snapshots of images and objects. A 360°screen in the center of the pavilion brings a fantastic virtual experience of flying, swimming and roaming the streets of Istanbul.

EXPO 2010

240

Ukraine Pavilion

The exhibition is to display Ukraine's past farming culture, today's modern culture and its future urban architecture. Trigram-like wall decorations in red, black and white originate from the symbol of an ancient tribe. Snake symbolizes the passage of time and change of seasons. Dog means the force to drive away the evil and Sun is a symbol of endless power.

Carpathian State National Park, Europe's largest national forest park and one of Ukraine's seven natural wonders, is exhibited to show Ukraine's efforts to increase the vitality of eco-environment in cities. Folkloric performances and live shows of traditional processes of making ceramics, embroidery and woodcuts are presented. Visitors can also try making color eggs or pottery jars in the pavilion.

上海
世博会

UK Pavilion

Theme
Building on the Past, Shaping Our Future

Zone	National Day	Year	Month	Day
C		2010	9	8

The UK Pavilion encourages visitors to look at the role of nature and wonder whether it could be used to meet the social, economic and environmental challenges of our cities. The dandelion-shaped Seed Cathedral, centerpiece of the pavilion, is covered with 60 000 crystalline spines that are tipped with tiny lights. They illuminate the pavilion during the day and make the whole structure glitter at night.

The UK Pavilion is separated into several parts of Green City, Open City, Seed Cathedral, Living City and Open Park. Green City presents the urban landscape of the four UK provincial capitals. The UK has a rich tradition of incorporating green spaces and water into its cities. Seed Cathedral exhibits seeds of different shapes and types from Kew's Millennium Seed Bank collection. Living City exhibits real and imaginary plants. These exhibitions show UK's creativity, high-tech achievements as well as its vision about how a future city will interact harmoniously with nature and be empowered by technological innovations.

The pavilion design resembles the wings of an eagle extending out to welcome visitors, also symbolizing strength, courage, freedom and immortality. Apart from the waterfall media wall outside the pavilion, the ecological roof garden highlights sustainable urban construction technologies.

The pavilion deals with the theme from four aspects, presenting the country's culture, values, innovation spirit and business success, showing incentives to individuals and capability in community improvement, and praising freedom, diversity, innovation and opportunity. Through multimedia technologies, it tells an ordinary American's view of innovation and community development and depicts American's hope for future. The exhibition on achievements of Chinese Americans includes a wall erected in recognition of the outstanding contributions made by Chinese Americans.

上海
世博会

Venezuela Pavilion

Theme
Better Life, Better City

Zone	National Day	Year	Month	Day
C		2010	7	5

Venezuela hopes to improve people's life, including those living outside cities in a traditional sense, as accepting diverse lifestyles is essential for harmonious urban life. The pavilion assumes a 3D pattern known as "Klein Bottle", i.e. a boundless and continuous curved surface where there is no clear cut between the inside and the outside so that visitors might find themselves outside just after turning around a corner. Amazing changes convey the idea of "solidarity, living together, balance" and respect for environment.

Ascending steps represent obstacles in the path of integrating into the mainstream society, indicating Venezuela's pursuit of diversity, inclusiveness and integration. A fusion of characteristic elements such as open-air courtyard, living space of indigenous inhabitants and Bolivar Square create a poetic picture and present both collision and respect between diverse cultures in Venezuela. Simón Bolívar Youth Symphony Orchestra performs in the music hall. The screens in the hall show real-life scenes in Venezuela while Venezuelan citizens can also view the pavilion exhibitions and activities on a real-time basis.

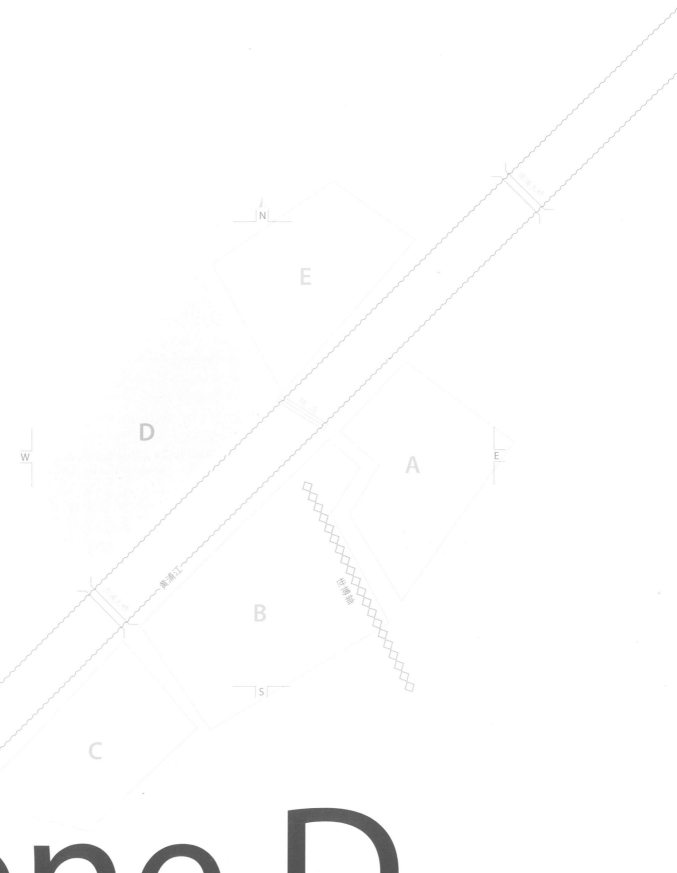

Zone D

246

Aurora Pavilion

Theme

Chinese Jade Culture,
New City Styles

Zone	Day of Special Events	Year	Month	Day
D		2010	10	16

Design of the pavilion is inspired by Confucius who suggests the eleven virtues of jade, which was summarized into five later, namely benevolence, righteousness, etiquette, wisdom, and faithfulness. The pavilion takes the shape of L, the initial letter of the phonetic transcription of a Chinese character meaning "courtesy and integrity". Mainly colored ivory white, it looks like a large precious jade. The two 6-meter-high jade statutes on the roof, modeling after Hongshan Jade Figure, are like the guardians and observers of Chinese jade culture.

Visitors can have close contact with three robots named Aurora Boys and watch a 3D movie on *The Goddess, Who Patches the Hole in the Sky*. A 2.5-ton jade carving finished in the 1960s and dozens of jade wares from Aurora Museum's collection are exhibited. Traditional jade making techniques are also presented to visitors.

上海
世博会

China Railway Pavilion

Theme
Railway Brings Better Life

Zone	Day of Special Events	Year	Month	Day
D		2010	10	2

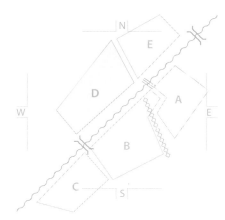

Mankind has created one wonder after another in the development of railway. The exterior design of the pavilion uses metal and glass curtain walls to represent the city, and panchromatic LED lamps to represent railway networks, showcasing the important role of railway in bringing a better life.

Railway, the bridge between man and city and between cities, injects more vitality into the city and brings people hope for a better life in the future. The first exhibition section displays the latest progress of China's railway sector with exhibits. The second section uses images to showcase the course of the sector's development over the years. The third section features interaction with visitors through models and devices.

上海
世博会

Oil is the blood of industry and fuels the growth of a city. The pavilion's exterior is composed of interwoven oil pipelines like a huge energy processing network, showcasing the efforts of the oil industry in extending city dreams and indicating the indispensible role of oil in future urban development.

The 4000m² exterior wall, made of a new type of green oil derivative PC plates, can turn into a super large LED screen amid the sound of fountain music at night. In a journey through time and space in the pavilion, visitors get to fully understand the role of oil in the progress of human civilization and urban development. Divided into the front, major, and rear exhibition areas, the pavilion aims to present in various ways the evolution of oil and its role in urban development, both in the past and in the future.

Cisco Pavilion

Theme
Smart + Connected Life

Zone
D

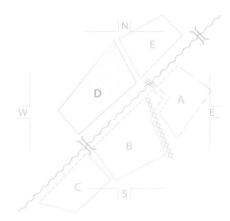

Technology is making communication easier and the world more harmonious. The pavilion is designed to show the good life at present and better life in the future. Technological progress is changing the daily life of residents in urban communities.

Cisco is working to create a smart and connected life by providing innovative technologies for sustainable urban development and digitalization.

A telepresence-based tour of "smart + connected life" starts with the warm welcome from virtual receptionist, an information wall showing a world where people are connected by technology. Movie *2020* is about family, friendship and hope, interpreting how technology may change people's life, work and study. The tour ends up with a review of the best moments in the movie, amazing visitors again with the power of technology.

EXPO 2010

Coca Cola Pavilion

Theme

Coca-Cola and Expo 2010, a World Refreshed with Happiness

Zone	Day of Special Events	Year	Month	Day
D		2010	5	8

Coca-Cola bottle show gives visitors unique sensation and extraordinary performances are presented on the unique stage. The pavilion's exterior is composed of water-proof metal shutters colored Coca-Cola red. In the Coca-Cola theater, a special video clip is played to help visitors better understand the theme of the pavilion that human beings have been pursuing a more positive, healthy, eco-friendly and happier life.

The pavilion is divided into five parts: Outdoor Show of Coca-Cola Bottles, Theater, Exhibition Hall, VIP Lounge and Experience Area. The aim is to present visitors a healthy and happy life and promote people's green awareness. Exhibitions on healthy drinks and innovation help to better interpret the theme of the pavilion.

上海
世博会

Japan Industry Pavilion

Theme

Better Life from Japan

Zone D

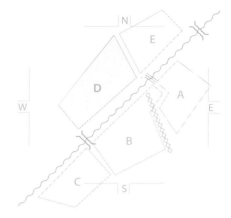

EXPO
2010

The pavilion, marked by red Mount Fuji, has a mesh structure of 10 000 pipes joined by 10 000 screw nuts and presents a pretty, lovely and agreeable Japan through the stress on the conceft of Reuse, Dynamics and Services in the design. The use of light steel pipes helps to cut CO_2 emissions by 500t. The theme theatre is decorated with recyclable paper tubes and pavilion staff wear uniforms made of renewable materials. Green awareness can be seen everywhere in the pavilion. On the west steel-pipe side wall, 130cm-tall robots present visitors great shows.

The pavilion consists of a theme theatre, eight main exhibition sections, stores and restaurants. In the main exhibition section, all images, sound effect and lighting change every four minutes and visitors may move ahead in response to the change in the last minute. In the theme theatre, a 6-minute movie *UTAGE* on Japan's culture is played in loop on an 18m-high and 10m-wide high-definition screen.

252

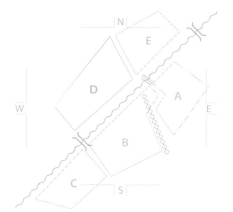

Insurance is indispensible to the sound urban development and betterment of human life. The pavilion is a single-storey building with a sloping roof whose main structure is the PICC logo and the exterior is colored bright white and red, creating an image of a reliable escort. Arch-shaped glass door leads visitors to the exhibition space.

The pavilion includes one axis, two wings and three areas, showcasing the functions and roles of the modern insurance industry in promoting socioeconomic development, progress of human civilization and safeguarding people's wellbeing with various technologies and exhibits.

Republic of Korea Business Pavilion

Theme
Green City, Green Life

Zone
D

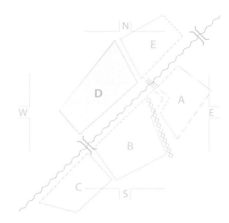

Inspired by traditional Korean Hat Dance, the pavilion takes a spiral shape of ripples, symbolizing the ties between human, environment, and civilization and echoing the theme by connecting businesses with people and cities with nature. At night, the spiral shines alternately in green, red, yellow, white, and black colors. Artificial snow falls outside the pavilion three times a day for 20~30 minutes each time. After the Expo, the pavilion's exterior is to be made into environment-friendly shopping bags for Shanghai citizens.

Exhibitions are about green technologies closely related with urban life such as cutting-edge IT technology and energy recycling technology. In the exhibition area on the 2nd floor, visitors can have a walk and enjoy easy life brought by hi-technologies through the 4D screens on the spiral slopes. In the Smart Home area on the 3rd floor, visitors can experience the intelligent elements of life, e.g. remote control of home appliances.

254

Shanghai Corporate Pavilion

Theme

My City, Our Dreams

Zone	Day of Special Events	Year	Month	Day
D		2010	5	4

Named "Magic Cube", the pavilion is an intelligent and interactive eco-building, whose design is inspired by a traditional idea on harmony in Chinese Daoism, i.e., Unity of Heaven, Earth and Mankind, and the romantic Zhuang Zhou's philosophical butterfly dream. A 15-minute interactive tour in the pavilion can inspire all those who have faith in Shanghai's future to play a part in its development. A 15-minute lighting and music show every night makes the Magic Cube more dynamic.

High-tech industrial robots welcome visitors at the entrance of the Magic Cube. In the 360° panorama theater, visitors are led by Prof. Butterfly to a fantastic tour of interactions featuring sound, light, electricity and image. Lastly, "delicious food" prepared by robots are presented to visitors, arousing their aspiration for future life. The pavilion roof is equipped with 2 200m² solar panels which ensures power supply for the operation of the pavilion. The plastic tubes which constitute the exterior of the pavilion are to be recycled after the Expo. Rainwater during the Expo is to be recycled for daily use or cooling the pavilion.

上海
世博会

Space Home Pavilion

Theme

Harmonious Cities, People and Space

Zone	Day of Special Events	Year	Month	Day
D		2010	10	15

Merely supported by columns, the pavilion looks like a suspending magic cube in the immense universe, arousing people's passion for space exploration. The fantastic design carries abundant information on technology, energy and space. The exhibition centers around the idea of "Heaven—outer space", "Earth—homes in cities" and "People—the subject to explore the space and build harmonious home" to show the role of aerospace and electronic technologies in urban development and improvement of human life.

Visitors can have a tour of fun, discovery and reflection in the pavilion. The prelude section Origin of Dreams arouses visitors' expectation for the future. In the theater of Spacewalk, visitors are told a story about man and space. The Beautiful Home section consists of a space scenario embodying Round Heaven and a scenario of future intelligent city embodying Square Earth, indicating that the ultimate goal of space exploration is to make the urban life better.

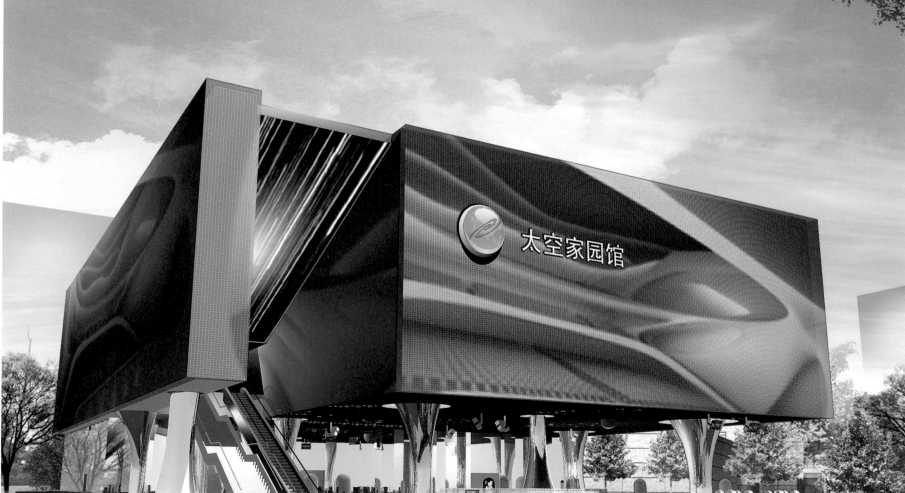

EXPO 2010

State Grid Pavilion

Innovation Empowers Dreams

Zone	Day of Special Events	Year	Month	Day
D		2010	7	26

The future of city is bound to rely on electric power and electricity-driven innovations. The central part of the pavilion is an Energy Cube which shines day and night. The lattice, alternately rough and fine, both actual and virtual, symbolizes the texture of city and the safe, quality, clean, and reliable power grid as well as its innovative approaches.

The theme is interpreted in a vivid and creative manner. A 12-lense solar light import device is used to provide lighting for the basement and VIP reception area. Solar photovoltaic power generation and lighting systems are used to display the sustainable development of urban power grid. The round holes on the exterior are simple devices for natural lighting. The crystal Energy Cube is a huge hexahedron immersing visitors in an audio and visual tour. Beneath it is the Heart of Energy, a high-tech substation supporting the Expo Site and all the pavilions.

上海
世博会

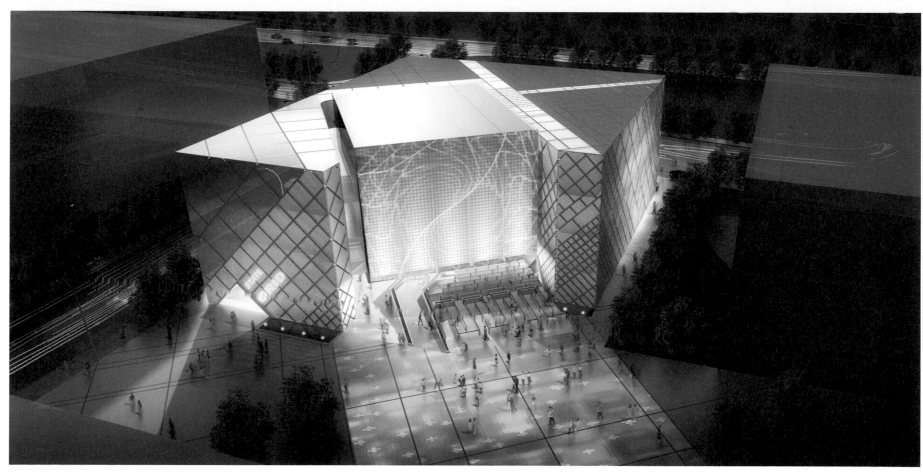

Zone E

EXPO
2010

Broad Pavilion

Theme
Direction

Zone	Day of Special Events	Year	Month	Day
E		2010	6	5

The pavilion, a white pyramid-shaped structure, consists of three parts of the Demonstration Building, Triangle Hall and Outdoor Direct-fired Heater. It takes just one day to finish the Demonstration Building, a unique exhibit for the Expo. Exhibitions focus on low-carbon and healthy lifestyle and the role of technology in environmental protection. Artistic expressions, multimedia imaging and multidimensional representation are employed to create great visual impact of the pavilion as a whole.

In the Triangle Hall, a giant simulated globe, suspended in the air, is to showcase the scenes on global climate change. Nine image boxes of various styles are to display nine themes about environmental protection and relevant images. In the center of the outdoor square stands a direct-fired heater, part of which can display the ongoing operation in the machine. Visitors can touch the machine and watch closely how fire is used for cooling.

上海
世博会

China Aviation Pavilion

Aviation Connects Cities around the World

Zone	Day of Special Events	Year	Month	Day
E		2010	9	21

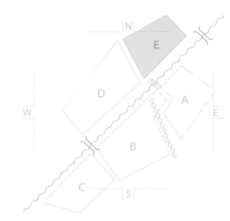

The cloud-shaped pavilion is covered by a white PVC membrane structure. As an important feature of its environment-friendly design, air is allowed in between its double roofs to improve insulation. When viewed afar, the pavilion also resembles extending wings of airplanes, implying the long-cherished human dream of flying and infinite opportunities for the aviation industry.

In the main exhibition section, a modern 4D exhibition system provides visitors with a thrilling ride, traveling across the vast forests against thunder and lightning and then returning safe and sound to a city. Visitors can also pilot a plane in the flight simulator area. It is noteworthy that wheelchair-accessible passages and routes are provided for the disabled.

262

CSSC Pavilion

Better Ship, Better City

Zone	Day of Special Events	Year	Month	Day
E		2010	6	3

Built on the site of the former Jiangnan Shipyard, the pavilion is like a boat carrying Chinese nation's hope for a better future. It has an arc structure resembling ship keel and dragon's backbone, symbolizing the indomitable spirit of Chinese national industry. The display of shipbuilding process and future ships probes into the future "water world" and the new pattern of human civilization. New green and multimedia technologies are applied to review China's long history of shipbuilding and highlight the prospect of Chinese shipbuilding industry. Visitors can make ship models they like simply by a touch on the screen, experience the life in a future water city, and feel the close ties between human, shipping and cities.

上海
世博会

Information and Communications Pavilion

Theme

Information and Communication
— Extending City Dreams

Zone	Day of Special Events	Year	Month	Day
E		2010	5	17

The universal coverage of IT technologies in the future will benefit cities greatly. The pavilion is in a streamlined shape without a corner, symbolizing infinite communication in the future, and its cellular appearance indicates the cell technology of mobile communication. The exterior is illuminated with changing color patches and light bands to create a sparkling visual effect. Main building materials are environment-friendly and recyclable.

Visitors can use cell phones to join in activities in the Dream Garden in the outdoor waiting area. Inside the pavilion, an amazing theatre presents a visually compelling picture of information technology and boundless communication of tomorrow. Visitors can use portable terminals to talk with iconic figures in the history of communication industry and interact with virtual characters in the Dream Theatre, and then they may look into the IT technology-based city life in a decade or more ahead.

Private Enterprises Pavilion

Theme

Vigour Matrix

Zone	Day of Special Events	Year	Month	Day
E		2010	9	5

The pavilion's design, inspired by "cell", perfectly embodies its theme. The growth of small cells into a huge living organism implies a similar evolving process of private enterprises. Composed of several large cylinders, the pavilion resembles a "cell cluster", symbolizing the union of 16 Chinese private enterprises. "Intelligent film" used in the exterior can produce different visual effects as viewing angles change.

High technology is used to tell the true story about the growth of private enterprises, showing the multiplier effect created by their union; a series of interactive activities are held to highlight the vitality and potential of Chinese private enterprises; exhibitions in such fields as computer and internet showcase the creativity of private enterprises and their contributions to diverse city life.

SAIC-GM Pavilion

Theme
Drive to 2030

Zone	Day of Special Events	Year	Month	Day
E		2010	6	12

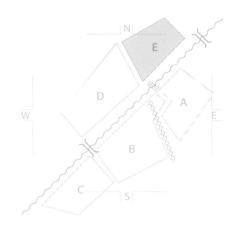

Inspired by car design, the spiral-shaped pavilion, like a sparkling angel's eye, symbolizes promises and progress and indicates the sustainable development of future auto and transportation industries. The use of environment-friendly materials is an important feature of the building design. Besides, leading-edge metal materials for the exterior, projection devices, LED and dichroic glass all inject vigor and dynamics into the pavilion.

A theme movie tells a moving story about transportation in 2030. Visitors also may write letters to friends, families or themselves and put the letters into the Post Office Box of the Future. 20 years later, these letters will arrive at their addresses. Besides, a huge arc screen with 144° viewing angle, 488 zero-delay dynamic chairs and newly designed concept cars bring brand new experiences to visitors.

Seven cylinder-shaped buildings made of wheat straw boards stand on the west bank of Huangpu River, symbolizing health and vitality. The low-carbon building probes into the possibilities of respect between human, nature and cities and perfectly embodies the concept of energy saving and environmental protection by reducing the energy consumption to the minimum. Its nickname, "2049" (the 100th anniversary of PRC), implies the future of an individual, a city, a country and even the whole planet.

The pavilion has five halls, each telling a story about respect. The termites' nest in the Adventure to Termitary hall gives inspiration to bionic architectures; the Respect • Possibility hall reminds people of cherishing gifts from nature; Tree of Life hall shows that people should make their minds to protect the environment; Mobius Band hall reveals the respect to nature in urban life; Elf of Snow Mountain hall depicts the vision of respect between man and nature via the story of golden monkeys.

上海
世博会

Urban Best Practices Area (UBPA)

Zone E

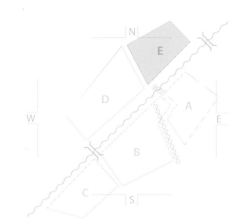

UBPA is to showcase recognized innovative practices of representative cities around the world to improve the quality of urban life and serves as a platform for cities to share experience in urban construction and development.

The Organizer of Expo 2010 sets up an International Selection Committee to choose the practices from over 100 cases from around the world on livable cities, sustainable urbanization, conservation and utilization of cultural heritage and technological innovations in built environment which are worth exhibiting and promoting.

UBPA is divided into the northern, central and southern parts. Built cases are exhibited in the simulated urban block in northern part on a scale of 1:1, so that visitors can experience better urban life of the future. Cases in pavilion are exhibited in reconstructed workshops in the central part to share the experience in urban construction with visitors. Other cases are displayed in the southern case presentation halls in the forms of presentations, seminars, networks, display boards, events and performances.

EXPO 2010

Built Cases (Northern Part)

Alsace Case Pavilion

Case Title
WaterSkin House

Zone **E** Built Cases (Northern Part)

The prototype of the case is the solar wall of Bouxwiller High School in Alsace, a great example of using solar energy to keep interior temperature at a comfortable level.

In the pavilion, there is a closed zero-emission system to adjust room temperature by using solar energy. The water-skin solar wall, controlled by the computer, can open and close automatically as the outdoor temperature and sunlight intensity change, shading the sunlight and reducing energy use. There is a micro-brewery running on solar energy. Visitors can see the whole production process and have a taste of newly-brewed beer.

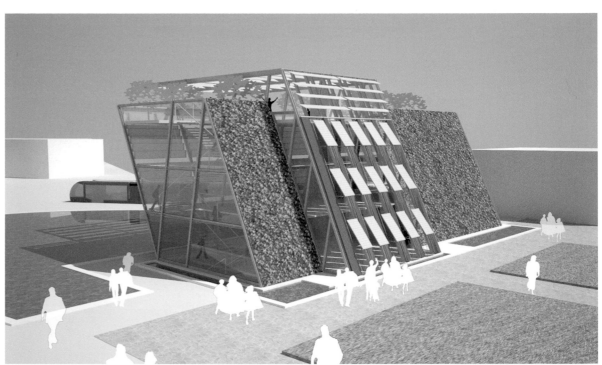

上海
世博会

Chengdu Case Pavilion

Case Title
Chengdu Living Water Park

Zone **E** Built Cases (Northern Part)

The Chengdu Living Water Park is a water-themed urban ecological park. Its design is based on the oriental philosophy that harmony between man and nature should be preserved and the ecological idea that man and water are dependent on each other. The park can collect rainwater and sewage, which can be treated and recycled through a natural water purification system.

The pavilion consists of an artificial wetland, a simulated natural community of local plants and local garden landscapes. It shows to people how the dirty and dead polluted water is turned clean and alive.

Hamburg Case Pavilion

Case Title
Hamburg Sustainable New Building Project

Zone **E** Built Cases (Northern Part)

The prototype of the Sustainable New Building Project is a building named H2O in Hamburg as both residential and office building. By using concentrated heating and intelligent ventilation, it becomes a passive building with low energy intensity. Cooling and heating is provided by renewables such as solar, wind and geothermal energy.

The 3D Wish Tree running through the entire building serves as a touring guide to visitors. Interactive programs help to give visitors a full picture of Hamburg Cities and sustainalbe lifestyle.

London Case Pavilion

Case Title
Zero-carbon Community

Zone **E** Built Cases (Northern Part)

It is a trend of the age to save energy, cut emissions and live a low-cabon life.

The prototype is the world's first zero-carbon community Beddington where every house has an open garden or balcony, combining high-density housing and comfortable life. According to the climate in Shanghai, the case pavilion reduces energy demand by installing energy-efficient facilities and achieves zero carbon emission by using renewables such as solar, hydro and wind energy. Visitors are presented zero-carbon auditorium, restaurant, showroom and six different styles of zero-carbon show houses built with green materials.

Macao Case Pavilion

Case Title

Restoration and Use of the Historical "Tak Seng On" Pawnshop in Macao

Zone **E** Built Cases (Northern Part)

The prototype of the case is the century-old Tak Seng On Pawnshop. In early 21st century, the pawnshop was rebuilt to be an industry museum through public-private partnership. The case is an excellent example of the preservation, restoration and use of the century-old pawnshop as Chinese cultural heritage.

The Expo Tak Seng On consists of the Pawnshop Exhibition Hall, the Important Figures Gallery and the Macao Archive. Multimedia is also used to tell the history of Tak Seng On and the story of its transformation into a pawnshop museum and cultural center. Besides, Jin Yong fans can find what they want from Jin Yong Collections.

上海
世博会

Madrid Case Pavilion

Case Title

The Sample of Government Low-cost Housing Estate

Zone **E** Built Cases (Northern Part)

The Madrid city council has been working on the largest public housing project in Europe over the last decade using green materials such as eco-technologies and effective construction processes. The most representative ones are the Bamboo House and Air Tree.

The bamboo house in Madrid is a five-storey residential building covered in bamboo. The Expo Bamboo House has various types of rooms to live making every visitor feel at home. Since the bamboo surface of different rooms opens in different ways at different time, the exterior of the entire building changes all the time. The Air Tree, right beside the house, is a decagon steel structure whose roof is equipped with solar panels for energy supply.

Makkah Case Pavilion

Case Title

The Tents City of Mina: Best Urban Practice for Extreme Conditions

Zone **E** Built Cases (Northern Part)

EXPO
2010

The Tents City of Mina, the world's largest tents city, accommodates over three million pilgrims every year in a 4km² area, successfully addressing the impact of such inflow of people on environment and infrastructure.

In the case pavilion, visitors are presented a model of the entire Tents City, the world's largest artificial reservoir on a panorama screen, the projects to protect the city from mudslide and flood as well as solutions to public transport, bridge and square upgrading. Performances are presented to visitors in the area between the entrance and exit.

Ningbo Case Pavilion

Case Title

Tengtou Village— Urbanization and Ecological Harmony

Zone **E** Built Cases (Northern Part)

The practice of Tengtou Village is the only rural UBPA case of the Shanghai Expo. Tengtou is a successful example of urbanized villages in China seeking to strike a balance between developing tourism and protecting the environment. The pavilion consists of several featured areas including Sounds of Nature, Close to Nature, Moving Images, Interactive Signature, etc. In the Sounds of Nature area, visitors can hear the sounds of different solar terms. In the Close to Nature area, visitors are exposed to the environment of Tengtou.

272

Odense Case Pavilion

Case Title
The Revival of the Bicycle

Zone **E** Built Cases (Northern Part)

Early in 1970s, Odense began to build cycling road and launch a series of bicycle-promotion policies such as changing the transportation culture, optimizing the functions of bicycles, etc.

The case is about the practice of Odense in promoting cycling. The exhibition area is like a sun face paper-cut in the fairy tale of Hans Christian Anderson. State-of-the-art interactive technologies are used to facilitate the participation of visitors. Various activities are held in the central area like opening a children's cycling school. A demonstration cycling road is built and traffic control facilities are set up to simulate real situation.

上海
世博会

Rhône-Alpes Case Pavilion

Case Title
Bioenergy & Sustainable Housing in an Urban Environment

Zone **E** Built Cases (Northern Part)

The prototype is an eco-building named INEED widely recognized as comfortable for work and life in the Rhône-Alpes region of France.

The case pavilion is a four-storey building made of recyclable baked clay. Staggered floors makes it for visitors easier to move between floors and survey all exhibition areas. The vegetation roof can purify air, adjust temperature, and drain rainwater in rainstorm. The rose garden in front of the pavilion shows visitors the most lovely roses in France. There is a business center, restaurants and a famous French cooking school where visitors can watch chef cooking and have a taste of authentic French cuisine.

Rhône-Alpes Lighting Case Pavilion

Case Title
Lighting Cities of Region Rhône-Alpes

Zone **E** Built Cases (Northern Part)

Rhône-Alpes has introduced innovation in urban planning, e.g. in street energy-efficient lighting. The Lyon government carries out a lighting project and brings unique features to historical buildings, urban structures and other public space. Saint-Etienne has implemented lighting plans in different districts based on the environment and infrastructure in the district.

The case is about the experience of the region in developing energy-efficient lighting system. Environment-friendly lighting technology is used to create fantastic night scenes. Different lights are put together to produce different patterns. One scheme is to produce firefly-shaped lightings which fly down and light up the Expo Site and stage a light show.

Shanghai Case Pavilion

Case Title
Eco-building Demonstration in Shanghai

Zone **E** Built Cases (Northern Part)

Zero-energy eco-building will be the mainstream urban architecture in the future.

The prototype is a demonstration eco-building in Minhang District, Shanghai, the first zero-energy building in China. Green and energy-saving technologies are used to collect solar energy and make the best of rainwater and sewage, natural ventilation, shallow geothermal energy, displaying the concept of sustainable eco-housing. The building has a shading system of shutters, French-window curtains and balcony awnings. Exhibition underground is to display the evolution of residential buildings in Shanghai and future intelligent living.

Vancouver Case Pavilion

Case Title

Legacies and the Livable City

Zone **E** Built Cases (Northern Part)

Canada is among the world's most livable cities, thanks to its proactive planning.

False Creek was where the Vancouver Expo was held and is now a most dynamic and attractive district in Vancouver. The southeast part of False Creek, the Olympic Village for the Winter Olympics and Paralympics in 2010, will be developed into the most creative, sustainable and passionate community in Vancouver. The case of Winter Games is presented at the Shanghai Expo to show Vancouver's experience in developing a livable city.

Xi'an Case Pavilion

Case Title

Daming Gong Relics Site: Protection and Surrounding Area Development Project

Zone **E** Built Cases (Northern Part)

The case, whose prototype is the three-*que* Qifeng Pavilion in the west part of the Hanyuan Hall of the Daming Palace, seeks to showcase the cultural charm of the relics site in Xi'an and sheds light on the harmony between heritage protection and urban modernization.

Visitors can take a travel through time and space which begins with visiting the beautiful Qujiang Scenic Area and then shifts to a fantastic 3D experience of touring the Daming Palace as it was 1300 years ago.

Cases in Pavilion (Central Part)

case	Case Title
Suzhou	Protection and Renovation of Suzhou Old City
Venice	Protection and Utilization of Historical Heritages: Urban Best Practices in Venice
Liverpool	Protection and Utilization of Historical Heritages in Liverpool
Cairo	An Integrated Model for Revitalization of Historical Cities
Hangzhou	The Water Control Practices of "Harnessing Five Waters" with West Lake at the Core to Construct "Quality Hangzhou"
Pondicherry	Achieving Economic and Environmental Goals through Heritage Preservation Initiatives as Demonstrated through: Asia Urbs Programme 2002-2004
Montreal	The Complexe Environnemental de Saint-Michel (CESM): A practicable example for the world
Bremen	From Knowledge to Innovation: Urban Transportation Solutions
Freiburg	Quartier Vauban – New Residential District for Freiburg
Guangzhou	Sustainable Urban Development — Water Environment Management
ENEA	Sustainable Italian-Style Cities
Rotterdam	Rotterdam Watercity
Sao Paulo	Clean City Project
Tianjin	Huaming Model Town — Tianjin, China
Dusseldorf	Business Meets Lifestyle — Livable City and Sustainable Development as Strategic Goals and Achievements

case	Case Title
Porto Alegre	Governance Practice Based on Social Consensus: Strategies for Social Integration Promotion
Ahmedabad	Urban Governance Initiatives of Ahmedabad
Alexandria	Alexandria City Development Strategy
Seoul	Seoul Culturenomics
Bologna	Bologna: Creativity & Inclusion in the City
Shenzhen	Dafen Village—the Regeneration of an Urban Village in the City
Prague	Morden City Protecting Its Heritage
Malmo	Urban Sustainable Development Projects in a Former Industrial City
Geneva/Zurich/Basel	Better Water, Best Urban Life
Osaka	A City of Good Environment: The Challenge of the Water Metropolis, Osaka
Bilbao	Bilbao Guggenheim Museum: the Leading Project in Urban Strategy
Paris	A River, A Scenic Spot, A Lifestyle
Beijing	Olympic Village
Barcelona	I : The Old Town in the Center of Barcelona
	II : The District of Innovation
Hong Kong	Smart Card, Smart City, Smart Life
Izmir	The Aqueducts Reconstruction Project: Sewerage Disposal Project
Taipei	I : A City of Resource Recycling
	II : Wireless Broadband — A City of Convenience

EXPO 2010

Other Cases (Southern Part)

Case	Case Title
	I : Sustainable Development of the City: Strategy and Governance
Ile-de-France(Pairs)	II : Making the Historical City in the Future
	III: Restoring and Developing the Legacies of the Sustainable City
Brest	Sea World Exhibition
Bonn-Bukhara	Energy Conservation Starts from Children
Luxor	Karnak and Gurna Development Project
San Francisco	Global Warming: A Case for Sister City Cooperation in Finding Local Solutions for National Models
Victoria	Classroom of the Future
Wroclaw	The City of Leisure
Rosario	The Management and Construction of Public Space on the River Shore in the City of Rosario
Hannover	Expo 2000 Exhibit "Kronsberg District" — Ten Years After
Yanbian	Green Ecological "Golden Triangle" in North-East Asia — Harmonious Family of Multi-nationalities
Dongguan	Engine of Sustainable Development
Guangzhou	Green Land Action
Foshan	The Foshan Mode of Transmission of Civilization — Foshan Ceramic Culture in the Past, Present and Future

Case	Case Title
Zhongshan	Charities and Harmony — Better Urban Life
Wuzhen	Wuzhen — Legacies Protection
Kunshan	The Four Charms of Kunshan, Eco-Orientation Inspiring the City Vigor
Yangzhou	Protection of the Ancient City
Zhouzhuang	Water Story, Water Town
Xiamen	Cozy City and Garden on the Sea — Xiamen "Livable Community" Impression
Tangshan	An Ecological Rehabilitation Project in Southern Coal Mining-induced Subsidence Area of Tangshan
Rotterdam	Rotterdam, Watercity
Hong Kong	Smart Card, Smart City, Smart Life
Bremen	From Knowledge to Innovation: Urban Transportation Solutions
Odense	Spinning Wheels — The Revival of the Bicycle
RHÔNES-ALPES	I : Bioenergy & Sustainable Housing in an Urban Environment
	II : Lighting Cities of Region Rhône-Alpes
Liverpool	Protection and Utilization of Historical Heritages in Liverpool
Barcelona	The District of Innovation

上海
世博会

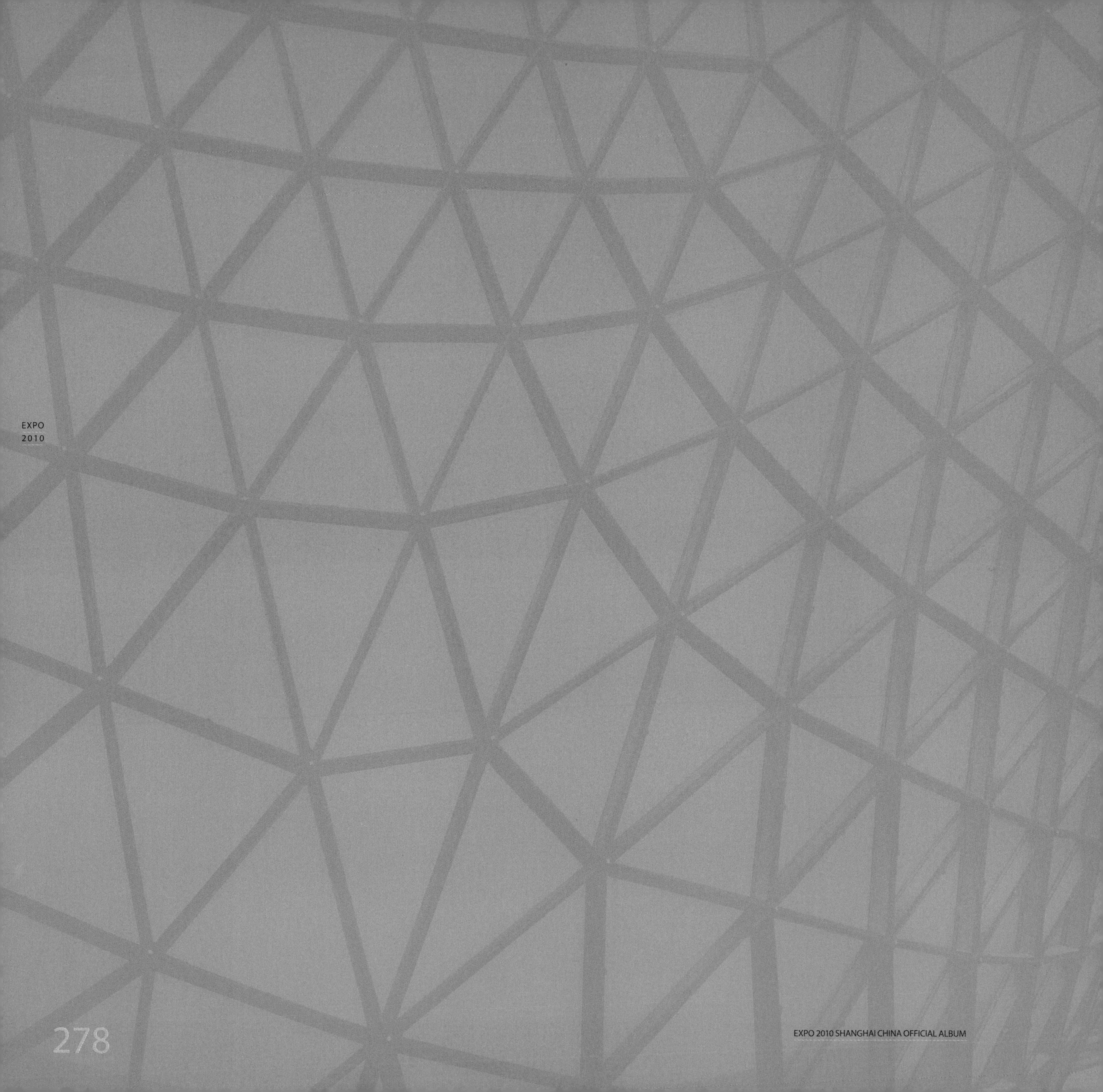

EXPO

Events

Over 20000 performances will be staged during Expo 2010. Artists from across the globe will gather in Shanghai and present performances of national flavors, displaying the unique customs of all nations.

Exciting and innovative events, as one of the three major parts (exhibition, event, forum) of the Expo, play a significant role in making the Expo "successful, splendid and unforgettable".

Events are either hosted by the Organizer or provided by participants. The 23 programs offered by the Organizer are broadly classified into ceremony, parade, stage performance and theme performance.

Twenty key words are used to describe the content requirements of the Expo events. They are theme, first performance, celebrities, local flavors, fashion, awards, street shows, art festivals, world intangible cultural heritage, cooperation, innovation, inspiration, Site opening and closing activities, intercity effect, creation, transmission, interaction, rationality, art exhibition and technological content.

Events to be held in Pudong and Puxi are defined as "Global Classic" and "Future Creativity" respectively. In addition to the anticipated Opening Ceremony and National Day of China Pavilion, many events are waiting for the visitors.

The theme show *Window of the City* to be staged on Houtan Square will be a highlight of the Expo events with its appealing plot, melodious music and strong visual impact. State-of-the-art stage design and high-tech multimedia, together with expressive body language of performers and their superb high-attitude stunt, will make the play absorbing.

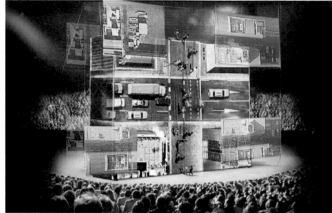

China Oriental Song and Dance Ensemble will stage a large music and dance show in the Expo Culture Center. *Colorful World, Splendid China* (both temporarily titled), will respectively feature music and dances of all ethnic groups in China and national dances from across the world. The combined modern concepts and classical elements, international features and Chinese flavors will surely make visitors thrilled.

Shaolin Kung Fu and Wudang Kung Fu, two traditional schools of Chinese martial arts, will be shown during the Expo. The Shaolin Kung Fu Play is a stunning show performed by Shaolin monks. The Wudang Taoist Kung Fu Mission produces *Wudang — Tai Chi Tao* to show Wudang Kung Fu, carry forward national culture, and tell the influence of Taoism on humanity, promoting the development of Taoist regimen.

上海
世博会

China boasts a time-honored history of tea culture. The acrobatic drama *Cha Show* specially designed for Expo 2010 will interpret the close relationship between tea and people via acrobatics, martial arts, dance, magic, music and Kung Fu, etc.

The Expo Site is also a paradise for the youth. "Abilia" experience activities, rod-puppet show *Journey to the West,* shadow play *Romance of the Three Kingdoms,* children's show *Magic Map of Sesame Street* and multimedia show *Haibao Is Coming* are both educational and fun.

The spectacular float parades, a dazzling array of performances, primitive jungle dances and gala shows in the Expo Site will dazzle visitors. The grand parades are a must see. As a cultural feast, the parades combine the themes of "Global Classic" and "Future Creativity" and are full of highlights.

Besides the magnificent events hosted by the Organizer, those offered by participants are exotic and rich in national flavor.

With a vast territory, China boasts a diverse culture with unique local characteristics. Folk art forms, stunts and unique skills across the country will be showcased during the Expo.

Breathtaking Wuqiao acrobatics from Hebei, Huangmei Opera and Fengyang Huagu from Anhui, Ansai Waist Drum from Shaanxi, Sichuan opera art Face-changing, Er Ren Zhuan from Heilongjiang, Zhoushan gong and drum music from Zhejiang, Jiangzhou gong and drum music from Shanxi, Yangliuqing Woodblock New Year Pictures from Tianjin, etc. will be presented.

Abundant folk songs and dances will be presented during the Expo, including Gal Laox from Dong ethnic group; Dance of the Golden Pheasant, wooden drum dance, and stool dance from Miao ethnic group; waving dance from Buyi ethnic group; bronze drum dance, Buffalo-fighting dance, lion dance and dragon dance from Shui ethnic group; dance drama, folk fashion show and wedding show from

上海
世博会

from Hui ethnic group in Ningxia; *Charming Xinjiang* and *Tibet in Heaven*, etc.

Other countries will also provide exciting performances.

Non-verbal comedy *Nanta* from the Republic of Korea combines traditional Samulnori Rhythm with kitchen to produce a comic show without a single word. Other Asian performances include *Two Thousand and One Nights* by Caracalla Dance Group from Lebanon, David D'or Concert from Israel, Indian songs and dances, song and dance parades from Nepal and traditional Afghani music shows.

The vast and magic Africa boasts age-old culture and art. Performance by Cameroon National Song and Dance Troupe, performance by Soweto Gospel Choir, Burundi drum show, shows by Kenya Culture Village, folk dance show *African Footprint,* and large acrobatic show *Africa Africa* are a feast for visitors.

Those fond of classical art will be attracted by the performance by Royal Ballet. Classical music lovers will have the opportunity to appreciate concerts by the Vienna Philharmonic, Royal Liverpool Philharmonic Orchestra and Teatro alla Scala Chamber Orchestra, and Scottish bagpipe show.

There will be a number of exciting shows jointly staged by Chinese and foreign artists. Besides, Salzburg folk troupe of Austria and Berlin folk choir will also bring thrilling programs.

Performance by Circus of the Sun

from Canada, Argentine tango and Brazilian samba will present unique charm of the Americas.

This will be a splendid and unforgettable Expo for people from all over the world.

EXPO

Forums

Forums

Of the three major parts (exhibition, event, forum) of Expo 2010, forums are closely related to its thematic concept and messages. They deal directly with its theme, and serve as an important platform to demonstrate the legacy of previous world expositions and to envision future ones.

Forums of Expo 2010 center on issues associated with sustainable urban development and interpret the Expo theme from a global perspective. In addition to exhibitions which demonstrate human civilization and innovative ideas, forums are held to discuss on hot urban issues and find possible solutions.

The forums consist of one summit forum, six theme forums and a series of public forums.

Summit Forum
Urban Innovation and Sustainable Development

Venue
Shanghai, China

Time	Year	Month	Day
	2010	10	31

The theme "Urban Innovation and Sustainable Development" reflects hot-spot issues of global concern and the development of themes of previous world expositions.

It will allow attendees to discuss on global challenges associated with sustainable urban development. *Shanghai Declaration,* an important document based on a consensus on global urban development issues reached by the participants of the Shanghai Expo, will be issued.

Chinese government leaders, UN Secretary General, BIE President, foreign heads of state or government, ministers, mayors, Commissioners General of Sections, and representatives from business, academic and other circles will attend the forum.

Theme Forums

Elite professionals from home and abroad will gather together to communicate on issues related to sustainable urban development and offer strategic proposals for the development of cities of all types.

The theme forums will be held in Nanjing, Suzhou and Wuxi of Jiangsu Province and Hangzhou, Ningbo and Shaoxing of Zhejiang Province and jointly hosted by concerned international organizations, ministries and commissions, the Executive Committee for the Shanghai Expo and the municipal government.

Theme Forum I:
Information Technology and Urban Development

Venue	Ningbo, Zhejiang Province

Time	Year	Month	Day
	2010	5	15~16

The rapid development of IT leads people into an era of information and makes informatization a natural choice for cities. The traditions and socioeconomic basis of cities are undergoing dramatic changes. The forum focuses on urban management, life and integration and envisions the future of cities in the context of informatization. It consists of a general assembly, three parallel sessions on macro aspects and four parallel sessions on hot-spot issues.

Theme Forum II:
Cultural Heritage and Urban Regeneration

Venue	Suzhou, Jiangsu Province

Time	Year	Month	Day
	2010	6	12~13

All countries, in particular the developing countries, should attach great importance to encouraging the coexistence and integration of diverse culture during urban regeneration and inheriting through innovation the traditional culture during urban construction. Cultural issues related to urban construction and development will be discussed from six perspectives, namely inheritance of tangible culture and preservation of intangible culture, integration of diverse urban cultures and cross-cultural communication, creative culture and cultural ecology, thus offering references for the cities of developing countries.

Theme Forum III:
Science & Technology Innovation and Urban Future

Venue	Wuxi, Jiangsu Province

Time	Year	Month	Day
	2010	6	20~21

Urban development and technological innovation always supplement each other. In line with the tradition of world exposition, Expo 2010 focuses on the harmonious coexistence of humanity, city and the earth, and pools the collective wisdom worldwide to develop the theme "Better City, Better Life". This forum will deliver its own explanation on the roles of technological innovation in safeguarding city security, driving sustainable development, enhancing urban competitiveness and creating better life.

Theme Forum IV:
Urban Responsibilities during Environmental Changes

Venue	Nanjing, Jiangsu Province

Time	Year	Month	Day
	2010	7	3~4

"Global Thinking, Local Action" has always been a slogan for environmental protection campaigns. Cities, as the breeding grounds for various environmental problems, suffer the consequences most directly. The forum centers on six topics: cooperation between cities in addressing environmental changes, comprehensive improvement in urban environment, green industries and innovation in production pattern, enterprises' environmental and social responsibilities, publicity and popularization of green concepts, sustainable life and consumption modes. The six parallel sessions stress the concerted efforts of government, enterprises and citizens in addressing climate change.

Theme Forum VI:
Harmonious City and Livable Life

Venue	Hangzhou, Zhejiang Province

Time	Year	Month	Day
	2010	10	6~7

People settle in cities for better life. While enjoying the enormous benefits of urbanization, urban residents also confront various problems. Centering on urban space, society and environment, discussions will be held on regional coordination, supporting systems, urban community, housing policies, built environment and social security to explore the relationship between harmonious city and livable life.

Theme Forum V:
Economic Transformation and Urban-rural Relations

Venue	Shaoxing, Zhejiang Province

Time	Year	Month	Day
	2010	9	9~10

Economic transformation is an issue confronted by most countries. Developed countries need to upgrade their industrial structures, while developing countries are under the pressure of the transformation from traditional agricultural society to a modern industrial one. The forum proceeds from economic transformation and urban-rural relations, and targets at overall social development. Discussions are held on economic transformation that has an impact on urban-rural relations as well as relevant issues on social development, to provide useful ideas for other countries, particularly China and India with large rural population.

Public Forum

Commencing in April 2009, public forums serve as a key platform to publicize and promote Expo 2010 which consist of the following forums:

Youth Forums, composed of a series of forums, is held both in China and overseas. Young people of different ages, regions and educational backgrounds gather to discuss the challenges they face and their roles in urban development. The forums can promote the influence of the Expo worldwide. The Youth Summit Forum is held during the Expo.

Forums of Provinces/Autonomous Regions/Municipalities are held nationwide. Each region selects one city (district) to host the public forum. Based on the "city" theme, topics for each forum reflect local culture.

Shanghai District Forums are held citywide. With the general public being the main participants, the forums explore the "city" theme and discuss issues concerning every member of the districts.

Culture and Media Forums are a platform where the public can actively participate in the Expo. It discusses issues specifically related to city culture, including cultural inheritance in the process of urban development, the role and influence of media, and the connections between popular trends and creative industries.

Women & Children Forums center on issues related to women and children as well as women's role in urban development.

EXPO

Landmarks

In addition to amazing pavilions, the Expo Site also boasts a number of landmarks, facilities and green space including Expo Center, Expo Axis, World Expo Museum, Expo Garden, Expo Culture Center and other important buildings for such purposes as conferences, performances, transportation, leisure and catering. These signature buildings interpret, in their own ways, the theme of "Better City, Better Life".

Expo Center

EXPO
2010

The Expo Center, on the north of the Expo Avenue and west of the Expo Axis in Zone B, will host the summit forum, ceremonies, VIP receptions and press releases during Expo 2010.

The exterior design of the building is simple yet elegant. With an impressive glass-curtain facade, it resembles a huge crystal palace. In the atrium of the Expo Center, the beautiful Expo garden seen through the glass-curtain facade serves as a natural background of the building.

As a venue for conferences, receptions and other events, the building is well equipped to meet varying requirements. Divided into Green Hall (central hall), Red Hall (auditorium for 2 600 people), Blue Hall (international conference hall for 600 people), Golden Hall (banquet hall for 3 000 people) and Silvery Hall (multi-functional hall of 7 200 m², used as main press center during the Expo), the Expo Center is a wonderful example of panorama buildings.

In addition to the elaborate internal design, the Expo Center also features the application of many energy conservation technologies such as solar energy, LED lighting and river water collection, turning it to be an outstanding example of green building.

Expo Axis

Expo Axis (1 000m×110m) in Zone B extends from the main entrance of the Expo Site to the Celebration Square and is the biggest structure in the Site.

With two stories above ground and another two underground, it is a semi-open building offering catering, entertainment, commercial and conference services. It is connected with the China Pavilion, Theme Pavilion, Expo Center, Expo Culture Center, and the elevated pedestrians' walk.

The Expo Axis is decorated with six inverted-cone shaped steel structures, the Sun Valleys, at its entrance and middle part. They allow in sunlight and fresh air, easing the feeling of oppression that may be easily aroused in an underground space and at the same time saving energy. Another attractive feature of the Expo Axis is the white "clouds" on its top, which make up the world's biggest stretched cable-membrane structure.

上海
世博会

Expo Culture Center

The Expo Culture Center, located in Zone B, resembles a UFO in shape. It may take on other forms from different angles and at different times. It is like a lovely sea shell in daytime and a floating city at night. Having two floors underground and six floors above ground, it is used for performances and some National Day events during the Expo.

As the first indoor venue with adjustable seat capacity in China, it assumes multiple functions. The seat capacity of its main venue can be adjusted between 18 000, 12 000, 8 000 and 5 000 based on performance demand. In addition to large celebrations and concerts, NBA basketball matches and international hockey games are also held here.

The stage, i.e. the oval part in the center, can be adjusted as a 61×30 oval ice hockey rink or a 28×15 standard basketball court. Besides, the size, shape and three-dimensional features of the stage may vary depending on the performances, which provide highly flexible solutions for stage design and artistic creation.

295

World Exposition Museum

The World Exposition Museum in Zone D has two floors and four exhibition halls. It mainly exhibits the cultural relics, historical documents and achievements of the previous world expositions.

In the front lobby, small-size replicas of over ten signature buildings of previous expositions such as the Crystal Palace and the Eiffel Tower will be exhibited. Made entirely of "gems", they sparkle brilliantly under lights.

Also on display are over ten types of Expo mascots, including Haibao, who are able to sing and dance.

The exhibition on history of world exposition includes precious exhibits at the first world exposition (provided by Victoria and Albert Museum), Ferris Wheel that debuted in the US, etc.

High-tech means are adopted to review the history of the world exposition and offer visitors superb and unique experience.

Bao Steel Stage

Located in Zone B, the Bao Steel Stage is one of the indoor performance venues for Expo 2010. Week of Province/ Autonomous Region/Municipality and other ceremonies will be staged. Reconstructed from old workshops, it has two stages and can accommodate 3 500 spectators.

An ingenious use of original facilities and environment friendliness figure prominently in the design of the industrial-building-turned-stage. Vertical greening is applied in the exterior wall of the stage to adjust room temperature; rainwater is collected from the roof to an underground impounding reservoir and recycled for indoor waterscape.

Thanks to its proximity to Lupu Bridge and its semi-open structure, the stage offers a wonderful view of the Huangpu River and the Expo Site. Indeed, it is a stage that can "breathe".

Entertainment Hall

The Entertainment Hall in Zone D is an event venue reconstructed from an old steel workshop.

It features a glass-curtain facade and a semicircle interior structure. The innovatively-designed red auditorium is encased in the glass lounge, like a diamond glittering in a crystal box. The roof lighting system evokes a dreamlike atmosphere at night.

The auditorium has about 1 900 seats. Side seats are not used for normal performances; and thrust stages will be built to meet the requirements of variety shows.

During Expo 2010, acrobatic drama *Cha Show* famous for its expressive body language will be staged here. Visitors will feast on martial arts, magic, songs and dances full of Chinese flavor. The Shaolin Kung Fu Play *Legend of Shaolin Monks* specially designed for Expo 2010 will also be performed here, which introduces to the audience the Shaolin Kung Fu and Buddhist meditation.

Bailianjing Garden

Bailianjing Garden lies in the north of the Expo Site in Pudong.

The Garden is designed around the concept of "rippling", which symbolizes a gradually-gained serenity after impact, integration after breakdown and calm growth out of cracks.

The tower crane in the crane square has witnessed the development of Shanghai as a port city and become a symbol of the city's industrial era. The eco-building half-covered in soil around the square and the curved steps form an ideal place for rest and assume the function of flood control.

The 1600m-long coastline of the garden and the reconstructed 13 docks on the opposite bank form a unique waterfront landscape. In addition to being used as yacht berths, the docks also provide a good view of the pavilions on the other side of the Huangpu River.

上海
世博会

Houtan Garden

Houtan Garden in the southwest corner of the Expo Site is a wetland garden.

The garden is dotted with various plants that blossom in different months such as peach, pear and pomegranate. Besides, crops that are rarely seen in cities are planted here to present attractive rural scenery.

It assumes the functions of wetland conservation, science education, water treatment as well as evacuation and rest area. Over 20 types of aquatic plants form a natural filter system that could purify river water without the help of any chemicals or specialized equipment.

Expo Garden

The Expo Garden is the main riverside green space in the Expo Site.

Drawing inspiration from "bund" and designed based on the environment-friendly concept, the Expo Garden rises from the bank of the Huangpu River and extends like a Chinese folding fan. Arbor trees on the upper level of the garden and roads, bushes, facilities and venues on the lower level are perfectly combined to make up a lovely landscape.

There are ten scenic spots in the garden such as "Wind Gallery", "Crane Wharf", "Arched Bridge", "Eco-stream", "Lupu Reflection" and "Beach Firs". The six precious Eastern firs are highlights of the garden.

Given the city's hot summer, the garden uses wind corridors, spraying, vertical greening and other technologies to create a refreshingly cool environment for visitors.

上海
世博公

Sculpture

Good sculpture is considered as the symbol of an era and the "totem" of a nation. As the "world language" among different civilizations exhibited at the Expo, sculpture offers a vivid and direct interpretation of the Expo theme.

A dozen of sculptures over the 5.28km² Expo Site will serve the functions of art exhibition, landscaping and theme development.

They will be mainly located in the Expo Axis, along the Huangpu River, and at main entrance squares and Jiangnan Square.

The sculptures in the Expo Axis are "Urban development should be in harmony with nature", "City should make life better", and "Art adds to the beauty".

Sculptures along the Huangpu River depict the hundred-year evolution of Shanghai and reflect the city's profound heritage.

Dynamic sculptures at main entrance squares, focusing on the theme of "festival", appear in groups and feature bright colors.

Sculptures at the Jiangnan Square with the theme of "Glory and Dream" trace the development of the city.

Besides, other sculptures in pavilions show the charm of art of masters. They include *Little Mermaid* in Denmark Pavilion, *The Age of Bronze* in France Pavilion, *The Angry Boy* in Norway Pavilion, and *Statue of Liberty* in San Marino Pavilion.

EXPO

Services

Ticketing

The Expo tickets are either individual or group tickets.

Individual tickets refer to standard day · single day admission, standard day · special admission, peak day · single day admission, peak day · special admission, 3-day admission, 7-day admission and evening admission; while group tickets are either group admission or student group admission. Tickets will be sold both before and during the Expo. In the three pre-sale phases, tickets will be available at a preferential price. The base price for an Expo ticket is RMB160.

Tickets will be sold through Expo outlets, designated agents, etc. The Expo Bureau designates some

Expo Site tour operators in domestic provinces for group tours. People interested may take part in the tours.

For the latest information, the public may access the official website www.expo2010.cn or dial +86-21-962010.

Expo tickets	Ticket samples	Expo tickets	Ticket samples
Standard Day · Single Day Admission			
Peak Day · Single Day Admission		Standard Day · Special Admission	
3-Day Admission			
7-Day Admission		Peak Day · Single Day Admission	

Catering

Expo 2010 is also a food fair for all the visitors. Delicacies from across China and the world are available at catering service points in the Expo Site, and restaurants are set in some national pavilions to serve specialties and snacks.

Many restaurants are opened in the five zones and the Expo Axis, offering full meal of Chinese, Western and Japanese styles, casual meal, fast food, etc.

The Catering Center west of the Expo Axis, divided into different zones serving cuisines of various countries, is the biggest catering establishment in the Expo Site.

Transportation

To facilitate visit to the Expo Site, Shanghai is building a comprehensive urban transport system and an Expo public transport network which enables visitors to reach the Expo Site via rail transit, bus and water. There is 1 rail transit entrance/exit, 8 ground entrances/exits, 4 extra-Site and 3 intra-Site water gates.

On most occasions, visitors can get to pavilions on foot in the Expo Site. Since the Expo Site is divided by the Huangpu River and there is quite a distance between the zones, the Organizer sets up a public transport system including rail transit, bus and cross-river ferry.

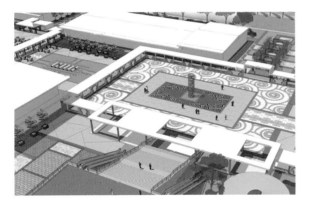

Shopping

The franchised products of Expo 2010 cover garment, stationery, gift, toy, shoes and hats, bag and suitcase, gold and silver commemorative coins, etc.

Visitors can buy unique Expo souvenirs and gifts in retail stores in public areas within the Expo Site. Besides, foreign countries also set up shops within their pavilions to sell souvenirs of national or pavilion features.

Visitor Services

To ensure that visitors have a pleasant Expo experience, the Organizer offers various services for the visitors, including information and reception, visit guidance, visit reservation, signage, rental, infant and child service, assistance for the disabled, lost and found, first-aid, etc.

Volunteers

The ingeniously designed volunteer logo resembles the Chinese character for "heart", the letter V (for volunteer) and a dove with an olive branch in its beak. It implies Chinese cultural element as well as the warm-heartedness of volunteers. The iridescent colors and steaming ribbons symbolize cordial hospitality of Shanghai. The slogan of the volunteers is "At Your Service at EXPO".

There are Expo Site volunteers and information booth volunteers. The services of the former mainly include information, visitor flow management, reception, translation and interpretation, visit assistance, and assistance in media service, event and forum organization. The latter are stationed in 2 000 information booths across Shanghai to offer services including information, translation, interpretation and first aid.

EXPO 2010 *Volunteer*

世界在你眼前，我们在你身边
At Your Service at EXPO

志 在 , 愿 在 , 我 在
My Will, My Help, My Pleasure

2010, 心 在 一 起
2010, We're Together as One

城 市 有 我 更 可 爱
Our City, Your Joy

EXPO 2010 SHANGHAI CHINA OFFICIAL ALBUM

EXPO 2010

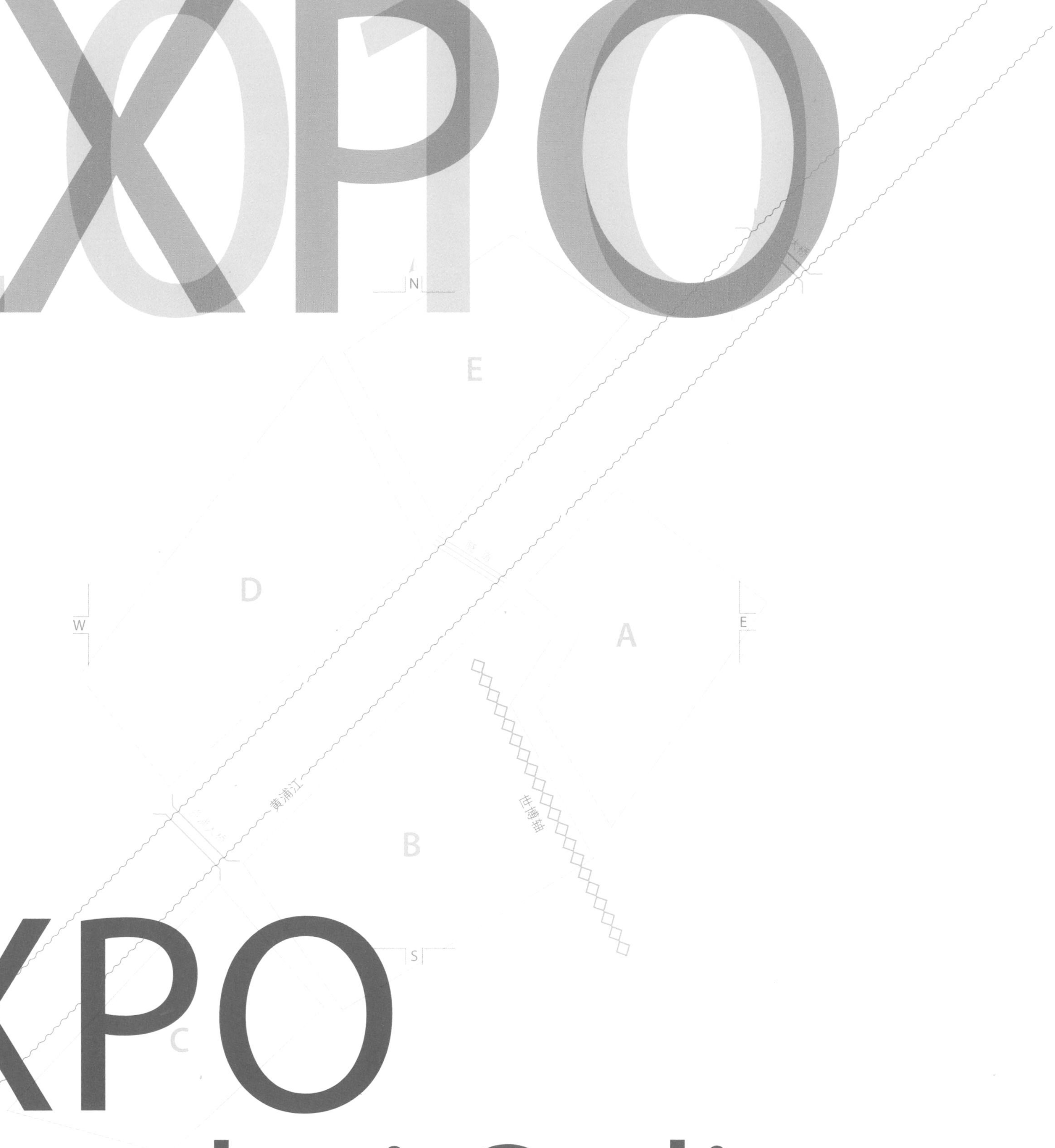

EXPO
Shanghai Online

As an integral part of Expo 2010 and its introductory channel, supplement and extension, Expo Shanghai Online is an online platform offering functions of promotion, tour guide, exhibition and education.

Expo Shanghai Online, a great innovation of Expo 2010, features a large number of audience, diversified means of communication and long duration.

It makes full use of the advantages of Internet and offers netizens the same experience as visiting Expo 2010 on site.

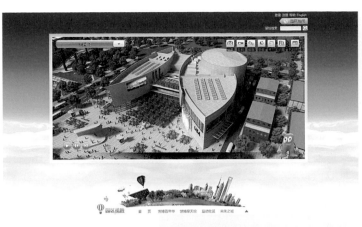

上海
世博会

It provides a three-dimensional and panoramic view of the Expo Site and pavilions, allowing netizens to tour the Expo Site and enter virtual pavilions to appreciate all exhibits and exhibition items.

The online pavilions are divided into Browsing Pavilions and Experiencing Pavilions. Browsing Pavilion offers an all-around view of the spatial layout and main contents in the online pavilion and an in-depth understanding of the exhibition items through texts, pictures, audios and videos. In the Experiencing Pavilion, netizens can get a more vivid experience via real-time interaction and 3D means.

"Site Tour", as the core of the Expo Shanghai Online, shows over 100 pavilions in the five zones and their exhibits and exhibition items three-dimensionally. Here, people can view a pavilion's exterior from different angles, tour around the pavilions and closely appreciate exhibits. And as an added bonus, some online pavilions would display a number of exhibits that cannot be found in physical pavilions.

"City of Future" is a 3D interaction and entertainment platform showing the most distinctive pavilions in the Expo Site. Netizens may embark on a virtual tour of the Expo Site and know the history of world exposition through interesting stories and games. They may also participate in building future cities in their own imagination.

In "Expo Ferris Wheel" there are interesting stories about the Expo, interpretations on the Expo theme and Expo movies; "Expo Carnival" offers Expo games; "Community" is where visitors can share their views on the Expo.

Publisher's Notes

From May 1 to October 31, 2010, the World Exposition Shanghai China 2010 will be staged in Shanghai.

To give a clear overview of the mega event, the Bureau of Shanghai World Expo Coordination compiles the *Expo 2010 Shanghai China Official Album,* which, with an abundance of beautiful illustrations, provides comprehensive information on exhibitions, events, forums, and other aspects of the Expo.

The book includes information submitted before March 25, 2010. Except for China Pavilion and the theme pavilions built by the Organizer, all the other pavilions in each zone are listed in alphabetic order.

Bureau of Shanghai World Expo Coordination
March 2010

EXPO 2010 SHANGHAI CHINA
OFFICIAL ALBUM

图书在版编目（CIP）数据

中国2010年上海世博会官方图册/ 上海世博会事务协调局编.

——上海：东方出版中心，2010.4

ISBN 978-7-5473-0161-6

I.中… Ⅱ.上… Ⅲ.博览会—上海市—2010 —图集

IV.G245-64

中国版本图书馆CIP数据核字 (2010) 第046830号

CIP Data

Expo 2010 Shanghai China Official Album/ Compiled by Bureau of Shanghai World Expo Coordination

—Shanghai: Oriental Publishing Center, 2010.4

ISBN 978-7-5473-0161-6

Ⅰ.China… Ⅱ. Shanghai…Ⅲ. Expo—Shanghai —2010 —Album

Ⅳ. G245-64

National Library of China CIP Data No. 046830-2010

Edited by Expo 2010 Shanghai Magazine

Produced by Project Team from China Publishing Group Corporation

EXPO 2010 SHANGHAI CHINA OFFICIAL ALBUM (Hardcover)

Compiled by Bureau of Shanghai World Expo Coordination

China Publishing Group Corporation

Oriental Publishing Center

(345, Xianxia Road, Shanghai 200336 www.orientpc.com)

China Translation and Publishing Corporation

(A4 Chegongzhuang Street, Xicheng District, Beijing 100044
www.ctpc.com.cn)

Issued by: Oriental Publishing Center

Printed by: C&C Joint Printing Co., (Shanghai) Ltd.

Format: 889×1194 1/12

Printed Sheet: 28

Insert: 1 page

Edition: First Edition in Apr. 2010 First Printed in Apr. 2010

ISBN 978-7-5473-0161-6

Price: RMB 230